Wiley Global Finance is a market-leading provider of over 400 annual books, mobile applications, elearning products, workflow training tools, newsletters and websites for both professionals and consumers in institutional finance, trading, corporate accounting, exam preparation, investing, and performance management.

www.wileyglobalfinance.com

WHERE DATA FINDS DIRECTION

*AT**Kearney***

To Howard Raiffa

May you always beat the global odds!

Paul A. Laudicina
Managing Partner and Chairman of the Board

Praise for
Beating the Global Odds

"With *Beating the Global Odds*, Paul Laudicina offers not only a provocative look at the major challenges of our time, but also the very real opportunities we have to convert headwinds into advantageous tailwinds. As countries, companies and individuals seek to solve the calculus for sustainable growth, this brisk and compelling volume by one of the world's foremost business strategists couldn't have come at a better time."

—Muhtar Kent, Chairman and CEO, The Coca-Cola Company

"Diagnosing the causes of decline is relatively easy. Inventing and applying remedies is a great deal more difficult. By drawing on a huge diversity of sources, by encouraging us all to become 'discerning omnivores,' and by applying the sum of his own peerless experience, Paul Laudicina helps us understand not just what needs to be done but also how to do it."

—Sir Martin Sorrell, CEO, WPP

"Seminarian, scholar, Senate staffer, from Chicago to the top of A.T. Kearney, from whiz kid to wise man: Paul Laudicina has written a book as singular as his career. *Beating the Global Odds* shows how to turn complexity into promise, and pixels into the Big Picture. Don't wait for the Next Big Thing; here is how to do it. The book is a concise and gripping breviary for the knowledge economy of the 21st century—the distilled wisdom of a thinker and a doer, a rare breed in the boardrooms of the world."

—Josef Joffe, Editor, *Die Zeit*, Hamburg; Senior Fellow, Stanford University

"This book is sensational. It is a must read for anyone interested in the process of innovation, and in the future of the global economy. Paul Laudicina uses a direct and personal style to transmit difficult—and sometime iconoclastic—ideas about a myriad of subjects. You will learn about complex systems, the comeback of scenario-based strategic planning, the need for expanding managers' peripheral vision, charter cities, and many other new ideas. After finishing this book you will see the world through different (and more powerful) lenses. But that is not all: this is also a very entertaining book. Once you start reading it, you will not be able to put it down."

—Sebastian Edwards, Henry Ford II Professor, UCLA Anderson School; Former Latin American Chief Economist, World Bank

"Business leaders often provide practical insights based on their experience. And thought leaders offer lessons based on their theories and analysis. Paul Laudicina is both a transformational business leader and a world-class thinker. With an engaging style, Laudicina blends in these pages the insights he gained from successfully turning around one of the most respected consulting firms with the best lessons management theorists and social scientists have to offer. This is an indispensable book—crisp, original, easy to read, practical and inspirational all at the same time."

—Moisés Naím, Senior Associate, Carnegie Endowment; Author, *The End of Power: Why It's Easier to Get, Harder to Use and Nearly Impossible to Keep.*

"Today's volatile, hyper-kinetic world requires fresh approaches to step back to strategize, to connect and to innovate. *Beating the Global Odds* is an incredibly rich resource to navigate you and your organization through the 'information smog' to new, clearer possibilities. Laudicina does a masterful job taking an extremely complex subject and making it accessible and useful. This book is a 'must read' for leaders globally."

—Kevin Cashman, Senior Partner, Korn/Ferry International; Author, *The Pause Principle: Step Back to Lead Forward*

"The world is getting more complex. We know that. We want to master this complexity but we don't know how. Paul Laudicina has done us a great favour by sharing tools and ideas to help us understand and steer our way through an even more complex and challenging world. Mukesh Ambani's foreword is an additional gift."
—Kishore Mahbubani, Dean, Lee Kuan Yew School,
National University of Singapore;
Author, *The Great Convergence:*
Asia, the West, and the Logic of One World

"Top-class decision-making in our over-complex, unpredictable world is an art. Paul Laudicina's new book offers highly valuable advice for shaping the future towards sustainable value generation."
—Jürgen Hambrecht, Former Chairman, BASF; Member of the
Supervisory Boards, Daimler AG and Deutsche Lufthansa AG

"If you aspire to lead and win, you need to get this book, read it, and give it to everyone on your team. *Beating the Global Odds* clearly and pragmatically shows you how to develop the mindset, passion, and relationships that drive our future—so that you can create what matters most in a world fraught with change and opportunity."
—Saj-nicole Joni, CEO, Cambridge International Group Ltd.;
Author, *The Right Fight*

"'Winning isn't everything, but wanting to win is.' Sage advice from the coach of the century Vince Lombardi. *Beating the Global Odds* shows us how to turn the desire to win into action—through concrete, pragmatic, realistic advice. Count me in."
—Kevin Roberts, CEO Worldwide, Saatchi & Saatchi

"*Beating the Global Odds* is a timely wake-up call for today's CEOs, who must work harder than ever to seize the opportunities—and manage the acute risks—that our ever-more complex global business and policy environment has handed them."
—John Quelch, Dean, China Europe International Business School
(CEIBS), Shanghai

Beating the Global Odds

Successful Decision-Making in a Confused and Troubled World

Paul A. Laudicina

WILEY

John Wiley & Sons, Inc.

Published by John Wiley & Sons, Inc., Hoboken, New Jersey.
Published simultaneously in Canada.

For general information on our other products and services or for technical support,
please contact our Customer Care Department within the United States at (800)
762-2974, outside the United States at (317) 572-3993 or fax (317) 572-4002.

Wiley also publishes its books in a variety of electronic formats. Some content that
appears in print may not be available in electronic books. For more information about
Wiley products, visit our web site at www.wiley.com.

Library of Congress Cataloging-in-Publication Data:

Laudicina, Paul A.
    Beating the global odds : Successful Decision-Making in a Confused and Troubled
World / Paul A. Laudicina.
        p. cm.
    Includes bibliographical references and index.
    ISBN 978-1-118-34711-9 (cloth); ISBN 978-1-118-41671-6 (ebk);
    ISBN 978-1-118-42030-0 (ebk); ISBN 978-1-118-43187-0 (ebk)
    1. Strategic planning. 2. Organizational change. 3. Decision making. 4. Change
(Psychology). 5. Diffusion of innovations. I. Title.
    HD30.28.L378 2012
    658.4'03—dc23
                                    2012022596

Printed in the United States of America

10 9 8 7 6 5 4 3 2 1

To my fellow partners around the world,
and the entire A.T. Kearney family,
who have generously set sail with me on our successful journey
together these past six years.

Contents

Foreword

I believe the book you are about to read is one of the most remarkable books you will ever come across. In terms of density of wisdom, the author has managed to compile it all into a concise and compelling package—giving you, the reader, an exceptionally high return on the investment of your time as you savor each page. In writing this book, Paul practices what he advocates: broad, multidisciplinary insight bringing simple clarity to a world of increasing complexity.

As for the man behind this book, I am honored to call Paul Laudicina a good friend—and more. My organization and its leadership have benefited enormously from Paul's wise counsel and incisive insights, not to mention his uncanny knack for having a pulse on almost everything. It probably was always going to be a difficult task for Paul to distill his wisdom into something so tangible. I am delighted that his book has achieved this almost impossible feat.

In leading a global institution of excellence such as A.T. Kearney, Paul has amassed tremendous learning over the past few decades. His ability to laterally connect issues and draw meaningful insights never ceases to amaze me. A vastly traveled, informed, and connected man,

Paul brings a wealth of personal experiences to all his dealings—at all levels. In the pages that follow, you and I get to travel alongside him.

Given the convulsions and changes the world is undergoing today, *Beating the Global Odds* couldn't have arrived at a better moment. As I write this Foreword, we are still trying to manage—and make sense of—the consequences of multiple global economic shocks. Nations that were ever so powerful and dominant in the past are grappling with sovereign survival. Nations that enjoyed economic supremacy are contemplating austerity. And nations that are ambitious and enterprising are on a new trajectory of finding their rightful place. This global reset has changed the world and has forced us to think in radically different ways to yield compelling, simple, and actionable insights.

Governments, corporations, civil society, and individuals all now have to reinvent themselves to beat the global odds, whether they want to or not. Business has a major role to play, not only to help provide stability but also to instill new confidence that the future could be brighter than the present. Paul also writes about the inescapable importance of values-based leadership. I have personally believed in values-based value creation in whatever we have done. Making a difference to the lives of millions of Indians has been a core value and driving force of my company since its inception. The foundation of radically innovating to fulfill unmet needs and aspirations of people has resulted in the fundamental transformation of whole industries. The rules of the game have changed, and sometimes the game itself has changed!

Given my own personal journey of enterprise and entrepreneurship, this book's insights have special resonance for me. The dictionary defines an entrepreneur as "a person who organizes and operates a business or businesses, taking on greater than normal financial risks in order to do so." This definition is inadequate in my view. I say this because I believe entrepreneurship is not just about risk taking for business. Entrepreneurship is also about risk taking for one's community, for one's country, and for the benefit of the entire world. Decision-making is not just about making choices. It is influenced by your ambition and what you are willing to sacrifice to make things happen. In every major initiative, we have tried to demonstrate the ability to think big, the ability to think of a large family of stakeholders, and the ability to think of our nation, and, increasingly, of the world beyond. For us, high stakes decision-making has always been in this context: high stakes for the broadest group of stakeholders.

Paul touches upon many requirements that may appear soft but are no less critical for success, such as the importance of relationships. We have always believed that relationships should come first whether with the broader group of stakeholders, with customers, or with business partners. Relationships based on trust and tolerance make efforts sustainable in the long run.

Paul also talks about information and complexity and the need to cleverly find the needle in an ever-growing haystack. We have always believed in decision-making based on first principles, which naturally clears up the clutter and allows us to focus on the most important requirements for success. Of course, perseverance and the courage of conviction play vital roles in this process as well. Sometimes the going has become tough, but our "no exit at any cost" approach has seen us through some difficult times.

Finally, Paul discusses strategic planning, especially through the medium of scenarios. We have always believed that a good strategy is only as good as its execution. What links the two is planning. We put unbelievable emphasis on getting the planning right. We develop a dynamic strategy emanating from a rich set of plans with fallback contingencies in place for course corrections, which will invariably be needed in this world of "continuous convulsive change" that Paul so rightly notes will be the steady state going forward. Envisioning the long-term future is a difficult task, but innate intuition coupled with astute and sometimes paranoid planning can help bring about the desired outcomes. Technology has fundamentally changed the way business is conceived, configured, and deployed. Big data is the next opportunity to harness intelligence and insights to help bring about exponential business growth.

We live in an ideas economy, and things change at breakneck speed. Planning thus needs to be a real-time and continuous process. It also needs to be nimble and agile, allowing the organization to take the right turns without stopping or slowing down. For that we need intelligent, committed, and mature teams with peripheral vision. Paul's latest book offers a compelling blueprint for such teams charged with delivering the future. *Beating the Global Odds* provides tangible advice for such teams to become extraordinary and world-class. Paul also offers an entertaining and inspiring guide to any individual who struggles with mastering the demands of a 24/7, 360-degree world of change, challenge, and opportunity.

Contrary to what some may think, the future *is* exciting and promising. I hope we all will beat the odds. Rather, I know we will—and this book helps us understand just how that is possible.

Mukesh Ambani
Chairman and Managing Director, Reliance Industries
Mumbai

Introduction

*Seizing the Future Is (Fortunately)
Not a Game of Chance*

As we begin, I can't do better than quote pioneering French aviator and author Antoine de Saint-Exupéry: "As for the future, your task is not to foresee it, but to enable it."
SOURCE: Fuse/Getty Images

If you're looking for a roadmap to a better future for your company, your country, our world, and your career and personal life, I trust this book will help.

Today's society—a swirl of businesses, governments, organizations of all kinds, and individuals—has been rendered confused and paralyzed by a multitude of shocks, crises, and high-speed changes that we are all more familiar with than we'd like to be. A technology-driven and connected world has exponentially increased our inputs and choices. At the same time, there is a lack of a fundamental, shared sense of purpose on which people and organizations can build things that last—inspiring and sparking actions that will yield longer-term benefits both within and across borders.

We can't, nor would we want to, turn back the tide of connective technologies. Instead, we need to leverage them to solve the very problems they helped spawn. Information Technology 1.0 has enabled a transaction-based society in which "the deal" became more important than the value it drove or the relationships it was based on. And so this decoupling of wealth creation from value creation is at the heart of today's increasingly angry, divided, alienated, and atomized societies. In this environment, individuals have retreated from integration, seeking refuge in the realities of their identity: nationality, ethnicity, religion. . . .

Yet, we know that narrow thinking impedes innovation. And innovation drives value creation, which in turn drives wealth generation. Wealth generation enriches business, government, society, and individuals. And we know that diversity of ideas and inclusion of people drive innovation, which in turn are extended by further advances in technologies that span time and space.

Only inspired leadership can help our post-Great Recession, atomized society rise above itself to realize a new, rising-tide prosperity. To inspire and compel purposeful action, leaders must be grounded in values—and be able to pragmatically employ the best of technology and new ways of thinking. This renewed sense of can-do pragmatism must help create the future by enabling it, complementing leadership with similarly thoughtful followership. Unless there is a deeper understanding of the consequences of inaction or improper action, the promise of daring to reach beyond the constraints of time and space to seize opportunity and manage risk will not be reached.

Today's leaders and citizens have to accept a world fraught with volatility and disruptive change, and they have to realize that inaction is not a good option. It's not all bad: This unprecedented volatility is accompanied by an equally unprecedented and compelling convergence of doing well with doing good—a blending of the pursuit of enlightened self-interest with the pursuit of the common good. Successful leaders will need to understand and act on this converging value proposition. By leveraging new technological capabilities and employing more dynamic ways of thinking and inspiring the future, we can beat the global odds.

Coalface Credentials

Coal mines are tough places to work, especially if you're working the mining equipment at the exposed seam of coal deep underground—the coalface. In Australia and some other places, the expression "at the coalface" means you're doing something, not just talking about it hypothetically or speculating about it from a comfortable distance. Given the nature of this book, I think you, the reader, deserve to know something about me before we get too much further.

I don't come from a traditional consulting background. A former seminarian, I studied political science at Chicago, worked for a large oil company, and entered politics before joining a think-tank and, much later beginning my current professional career in management consulting. Even in 1992 (the year I joined A.T. Kearney and founded the Global Business Policy Council) there were those who felt that an insufficiently technical and business-focused background was not a good fit for the hard-edged world of global business. Twenty years on, how much more difficult is it for a young liberal-arts type to enter the professional world?

On the other hand, technical knowledge becomes obsolete quickly, while the ability to think critically and write and speak well—the skills a liberal arts education provides—pays dividends for a lifetime. When polymath Mortimer Adler helped found the Aspen Institute in 1950, critics doubted that CEOs would have any interest in reading great literature and probing the "big questions," even in the bucolic setting of Aspen, Colorado. Turns out they were interested, as even business leaders of that relatively conformist era realized that technical and managerial expertise in one's industry was a necessary but insufficient basis for making sense of what was happening in the world—and for making sound decisions.

This book is about a journey—my personal journey, my professional journey, my firm's journey, my clients' journey, and, I hope, the reader's journey. I write this book in part to help understand and illuminate a personal and professional crossroads I have come to: As the saying goes, you don't know what you really think until you are forced to write it down.

I have spent a half century living in and being enriched by three worlds—a largely contemplative world of spirituality from my youthful years studying for the priesthood, which did not turn out to be what I was called to do; a highly inquisitive and externally engaged political world of my early career in government and policy-related positions; and a more mature commercial world working in business to help set strategic direction and meet corporate objectives for my clients and my firm.

These worlds often moved in independent and concentric orbits, almost as if they were governed by their own magnetic fields, coexisting without crossing each other's wake except under unusual—and often quite dramatic—circumstances. These separate and distinct domains operated in a relatively stable steady state of independence from one another until the wonders of technology began to erode the natural boundaries and borders separating these worlds. More generally, the forces of technology fueled the ever more rapid and cost effective movement of people, goods, capital, and ideas. These many forces in turn, broke the pressure lock separating all these worlds—making them ever more vulnerable and important to one another's ability to deliver on each of their own special missions.

A Quick Tour of This Book (and Why I'm Emphasizing the Renaissance of Scenario Planning)

I'll admit it's not enough to note that people and organizations are highly frazzled from the bumps, tumbles, growing complexity, and general overload of the past few years. Tell me something I don't know, you say? In Chapter 1, however, before we can decide what to do about it, we need to unpack the whole story a bit more. As we'll see, help is actually on the way, including from such (unlikely?) places as Santa Fe and Oxford.

In the two chapters that follow, I will take you on a series of visits to other sides of the complexity coin, including the ever-shorter half-life of everything, the increasingly messy and incapacitated politics of most countries, and the way in which our over-complex world has driven many ordinary people either to a state of angry populism or to just tuning out entirely. These trends are all closely connected and self-reinforcing in a negative way. To top it off, many of our brightest business minds have been given strong incentives to game the system, creating no lasting value and even off-loading risks and losses onto society at large. If this is capitalism, Adam Smith would find it unrecognizable.

So you might think, "Let's just wait until the smoke clears and the economy bounces back fully before committing ourselves to any definitive course of action." That might be an instinctive reaction to today's chaotic mixed signals, but I will advocate that inaction or staying in neutral would be the wrong choice—and a very big missed opportunity.

In the succeeding chapters of the book, I will give you a brisk spin around some remarkable ideas, places, companies, and people who are definitely not waiting for some Eldorado of boom times to reemerge from the ashes of the Great Recession. Behind the scenes, they are innovating like mad; lightening the material content of everything; simplifying and curating the interface where people connect with products, services, organizations, and governments; and repairing social fabric wherever relationships and bonds of trust have been frayed (which is pretty much everywhere).

In the final part of the book, I will try to give you a peek into where to prospect for new ideas and insights, how to use (and not misuse) expert opinion, why you should widen your lens of inputs in a discerning way, and, lastly, how and when to deploy serious foresight disciplines such as scenario planning—whether for professional or personal high stakes decision-making. As I will emphasize later, there is only one past and one present, but there are multiple possible futures for you, your organization, and our world. Happily, seizing the future is not a game of chance or fate, but rather much more a matter of skill and foresight—and thinking about the future in the right way is really about informing present decisions with a fresh sense of the possible.

Scenario planning, which was born in the Cold War period of thinking the unthinkable and later played a significant role in various attempts to make sense of economic turbulence and oil shocks, is enjoying a rebirth with corporations and governments as they try to anticipate what might lie ahead. After all, who wouldn't prefer fresh thinking and insights and a new sense of purposeful action to the alternative of staleness and shell shock? But scenario planning (or scenario-based strategic planning, as it might be better termed) is a real discipline that needs to be learned before it can be applied, much as you would need to learn accounting (or vascular surgery or in fact anything) before attempting to do it—or even before you become a consumer of someone else's scenarios. I will do my best to show you the way.

What's Different, What Never Changes, and a Tale of Two Cities

Reality is always more complex (and faster-changing) than any attempt to sloganize it—or to try to force-fit some paradigm or acronym.

When I was a university student, the work of pioneering psychologist and philosopher William James had a major impact on my thinking. James, the father of American pragmatism, recognized that you first needed to accept and believe something before you could bring some structure to your life and thinking (i.e., to make a leap of faith of some kind before you can act decisively). Pragmatism was the antidote to the rigid school of scientific materialism—the need to have empirical certitude supporting every decision. All this remains true: We are still trying to bring order to chaos, and perennial, universal questions continue to gnaw at us. Read (or reread) a translation of some ancient manuscript or papyrus (sacred or otherwise) from 3,000 years ago, and you will be amazed at how people's thoughts, hopes, and worries at that time look remarkably similar to what we think and feel today. This has not changed and probably never will. As Aristotle asserted over 2,300 years ago, "All human actions have one or more of these seven causes: chance, nature, compulsion, habit, reason, passion, and desire."

Some things have changed, though. What's different now is the level of complexity and velocity we are faced with in every aspect of our lives and occupations. In short, what has changed is the ramp speed. What has also changed (decreased, of course) is the level of engagement of large groups of the public, who feel (and are) adrift. The courage required to make a somewhat more difficult leap is more significant than ever, as are the eloquence and inspiration needed to encourage others to come along for the ride.

If complexity and speed have increased exponentially in recent years, there is help on the way, and in some sense it's a "tale of two cities": Two unlikely places—ancient Oxford and avant-garde Santa Fe—are providing some truly breakthrough ideas about how to tame ever-increasing complexity and make it work for us, and also how advances in scenario planning and related foresight disciplines can help us think about the future and inform the present in ways that classic forecasting, polling, expert opinion, and so on never did or ever can.

Santa Fe is an old place by American standards: It has the oldest government building still in use (the Palace of the Governors); the oldest church in continuous operation (the San Miguel Mission);

and it just celebrated its 400th anniversary—not to mention that this tiny state capital has the country's third-largest art market by dollar value after New York and Los Angeles. But in the sparsely populated high desert of Northern New Mexico with its brilliant sunsets, you can still re-invent yourself with relative ease. When the U.S. government resolved to pursue secret work to invent an atomic bomb during World War II, it decided to use Santa Fe as the staging ground for the even more remote location of Los Alamos, about an hour away. The Manhattan Project (as it was called) in turn forced scientists and government strategists to confront entirely new questions of life and death on a previously unimaginable scale: "thinking the unthinkable" in the words of Herbert Kahn of the Hudson Institute, whose work fed directly into the creation of scenario planning.

In the early 1980s, according to the history of the Santa Fe Institute provided on its website, a group of Los Alamos National Lab scientists felt a "general dissatisfaction with the stove-piped, bureaucratic, funding-centric approach to science that had taken hold both at the federal laboratories and academia. And each felt that this carrot-and-stick support of science was, on a massive scale, leading their colleagues toward scientific myopia, reductionism, and stagnation. Furthermore, they believed, some of science's biggest questions, those that required a more expansive perspective, were going unanswered to the detriment of science and mankind."

So the Santa Fe Institute was born as a stand-alone, transdisciplinary research institute. This was not an entirely new idea: 100 years ago when the world's top brainpower hubs were the 10 or so leading German universities, Kaiser Wilhelm II (despite his many faults) had the interesting idea to create an elite, stand-alone research institute, which survives today as the group of well-regarded Max Planck Institutes. In North America, the independent Institute for Advanced Study was created in 1930 near Princeton University and attracted luminaries such as Albert Einstein. But it wasn't until the 1980s and 1990s that the new Santa Fe Institute (SFI) established itself as one of the world's leading centers for research across disciplines and, indeed, in the vacant space between disciplines. Today, research and insights coming out of SFI give us hope that the complexity that is currently overwhelming us can be tamed and harnessed for good by use of the very instruments that have created this complexity. (I will tell you more about that later.)

As for Oxford University, it's on the other side of the time scale: It's so old that no one even knows the approximate year when it was founded. Teaching has gone on there since around 1096—the better part of a thousand years. But, as the saying goes, something isn't good because it's old; it's very old because it's very good. Unlike most universities that are relatively centralized and highly structured by school and department, Oxford remains an eccentrically assembled, loose confederation of independent colleges, halls, faculties, units, and centers of various kinds. Although it was very late to the business school scene (founding a business school in 1996, long after management studies had become respectable elsewhere), it has now carved out the world's pre-eminent niche in scenario planning and related foresight disciplines. Along with its sister university, Cambridge, it is the only institution that has managed to stay in the world's top tier for literally centuries—and is still going strong. But why? There are a number of reasons for Oxford's continuing importance, including its being an important intellectual focal point for the entire English-speaking world.

But there's more to it: Oxford's loose confederation means that the disciplinary stovepipes are less rigid than they are elsewhere. In Oxford's 38 separate colleges, marketing professors and poetry scholars dine with astrophysicists and theologians each night, over such delicacies (for acquired tastes!) as potted shrimp, reform cutlets, and orange fool. One well-endowed historic college (All Souls) has no students at all, only faculty members (known as fellows) who are given the gift of free time and staff support to use as they see fit. And, even as a very old institution, Oxford relishes the constant infusion of fresh blood. Cecil Rhodes' famous scholarship program has brought some particularly talented new blood to the place every year since 1902. One such person was a brilliant scholar and cricketer who came from the far reaches of Western Australia in 1974—Rod Eddington—who went on to lead Cathay Pacific Airlines and later British Airways.

Sir Rod (as he now is) came back to Oxford in 2003 to speak to a large group of Rhodes Scholars and Oxford MBA students. He reminisced about the place and about the essential need for suppleness in our thinking and action, to avoid veins that become clogged and a mindset that becomes crusty and sclerotic, and to demonstrate that doing well and doing good must go together:

> Whatever his faults, the basis of [Rhodes'] scholarship was selection on merit. Neither race, religion or need were to be taken into account. He counted moral qualities as well as intellectual ones and admired the instinct for public service as highly as anything else . . .
>
> If history teaches us anything, and we can only hope it does, there is a way ahead that should be obvious to us. If the West is to retain its position, we have to be inclusive. . . . We must not make the mistake of thinking that everybody thinks as we do. There is tension between the centre and the edges, between head office and the outposts, between the World Trade Organization and the world's traders, from Calcutta to Qatar—that's the essence of organization, and I suggest it has some very important implications for our global [system] too. Unless those arrangements deliver unequivocal benefits for countries less powerful and rich than our own, we will start depending more on force and less on persuasion. . . . It doesn't work. . . . If we lose suppleness, we'll lose the game.

Chapter 1

Global Brain Freeze

Nonstop Overstimulation Brings Disorientation

If you're going through hell, keep going.

—Sir Winston Churchill

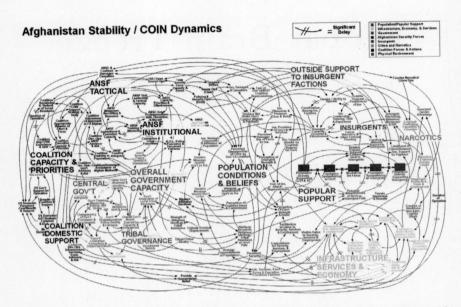

General Stanley McChrystal famously said in Afghanistan, "When we understand that slide, we'll have won the war." One might say we have met the enemy, and it's overload, confusion, and disorientation.
SOURCE: U.S. Department of Defense.

Y ou know the feeling: At the end of a long flight, the wheels touch down, and you instinctively reach for your iPhone or BlackBerry—pressing the on button even before the reverse thrust kicks in. Within about 10 seconds (if you're lucky), your device picks up a signal, and then the messages start streaming in, each one giving your already overstimulated brain a dopamine hit. Maybe if you've just arrived in Mumbai after a 14-hour flight, you've got literally hundreds of incoming e-mails, a dozen voicemails, and bad economic news to process and react to: Global markets may have plunged again while you were trying to doze during the second meal service. Perhaps you're grateful that aircraft don't yet universally have in-flight WiFi configured, or you wouldn't have gotten any chance to rest at all. In the sedan on your way to the hotel, you try to hack your way through some of the messages, answering those that only require a quick response and preferably little thought.

UCLA psychiatrist Gary Small's research shows that this continuous partial attention actually leads to a kind of brain fog, where much information is skimmed but nothing useful really sticks. You make a mental note to yourself: Does answering e-mail for 10 hours a day constitute productive work, or, for that matter, a productive life? Fortunately or otherwise, neither you nor I have time to dwell on that question. We need to keep rolling, one foot in front of the other.

More Has Become (Much) Less

I don't claim to be a prophet, and in fact I know I still spend far too much time reacting to incoming developments rather than anticipating

From crisis and scandal to the proliferation of product choice and the relentless 24/7 information smog of always-on news, e-mail, and social media, we are not feeling especially smarter or wiser. On the contrary, our ability to think and act decisively with the future in mind has diminished. Imagine having—at last—the entire knowledge of human civilization at your fingertips, and finding that it basically gives you a migraine.

them. On the other hand, in 2005 I authored a book entitled *World Out of Balance*. Despite the continuing halcyon days of economic boom, I took the then-unfashionable view that all was not well with the world and gave some specific advice about what business leaders needed to do to adapt their companies, and, more importantly, their thinking, to some volatile new realities. In hindsight, I wish I had been dead wrong about the future that would unfold. Seven years on, the pace of change has only accelerated, and rather than being brought back into balance, our world has undergone a further series of upheavals that have shaken us to the core.

Not surprisingly, people (and organizations) everywhere are feeling disoriented, bewildered, and even paralyzed. From crisis and scandal to the proliferation of product choice and the relentless 24/7 information smog of always-on news, e-mail, and social media, we are not feeling especially smarter or wiser. On the contrary, our ability to think and act decisively with the future in mind has diminished. Imagine having—at last—the entire knowledge of human civilization at your fingertips, and finding that it basically gives you a migraine. Michael Lederer, an American writer who lives in Berlin and Dubrovnik, Croatia (son of a dear, late friend of mine), calls this *Mundo Overloadus*—the title of his recent play that premiered in New York.

There is something you can do about it. But first, you have to understand it. You won't be alone, as a considerable amount of effort is being put into this endeavor by a number of innovative firms. One of the principles behind Google, for example, is to use technology to more effectively sort, categorize, and manage information on a vast scale. While Google is widely considered one of the most successful and admired companies of our time, even its current approaches to innovation may be nearing their natural limit. Sophisticated tools to track users' behaviors and preferences, and to match them with the closest content providers, have had the unintended consequence of limiting results to a too-narrow and self-selecting range, while clever companies have found ways to manipulate their own content so that it shows up higher in search results. Google recognizes this and is constantly attempting to update its algorithms accordingly, but one wonders if this cat and mouse game will go on indefinitely.

The point is not made to single out or pick on Google; it's a brilliant company filled with bright and creative people. Rather, the problem stems from addressing a new challenge with an old paradigm. The old paradigm tells us that as the volume of available information increases, the capacity of the organizational system adapts to accommodate it. Throughout history, from the Ancient Library of Alexandria, Egypt, to Gutenberg's moveable type-enabled printing, to the Dewey decimal system and the personal computer, and, now, to Google, this has been the case. Like competing Cold War adversaries, the arms race between the expansion of knowledge and the systems to organize it has historically been in balance. New tools, faster processors, larger data centers, and mobile devices connected to high-speed wireless data networks work behind the scenes to ensure that wherever you are, you are not left without a digital assistant. All these things have helped to make the immense and ongoing expansion of the world's body of knowledge an asset to leverage, rather than an albatross around the neck.

In today's world, however, this has changed, for two reasons. First, with the geometric expansion of available knowledge and the increasing diversity of ways to deliver and access it, we are past the point where new tools can be developed in enough time to keep pace—at least for now. The second is that, regardless of the capacity or technological sophistication of our tools (later in this volume I will discuss how technology is evolving to help tame technology), the volume and velocity of information increases geometrically, but our ability to

Effective leaders (or in fact effective people in any occupation) simply do not zoom at warp speed continuously. Finding the right time to pause, think, reflect, recharge, and be creative is absolutely essential to success in any field.

understand and act upon that information explosion chugs behind linearly. No longer can the information surge be managed solely through superior organization. Rather, a wholesale new way of thinking, behaving, and discerning is necessary to manage and cope with the pace of change and disruption. In a sense, this represents a new limit to the utility of technology—even the best systems will be limited by the capacity of individuals and society to usefully absorb the data surge and then, with wisdom, to know what to do with it. I'm not advocating that you cut your cables and smash your smartphone, although there are those intent on doing just that. Taking a page from Henry David Thoreau and his self-imposed isolation at Walden Pond, author and media analyst Dr. Thomas Cooper says that the only healthy response to *fast media* is a *media fast*—a kind of detox for the mind.

I think a better approach for most people is what Kevin Cashman, senior partner of big-league executive search and talent management firm Korn/Ferry, calls the *The Pause Principle* (which is also the title of his excellent new book). Effective leaders (or in fact effective people in any occupation) simply do not zoom at warp speed continuously. Finding the right time to pause, think, reflect, recharge, and be creative is absolutely essential to success in any field. In what Kevin calls our relentless VUCA world—an acronym for *volatility, uncertainty, complexity,* and *ambiguity* originally coined by the U.S. Army War College—we all need to find time to pause regularly in order to refresh our minds, bodies, and thinking and to take stock of things overlooked in the hubbub of daily life and work.

It's largely forgotten now, but the late German thinker Josef Pieper (he died in 1997) published a highly contrarian and countercultural work in 1952 called *Leisure: The Basis of Culture,* with no less than T. S. Eliot writing the introduction to the English-language edition.

Pieper's view was that everything that we value about human civilization requires surplus capital and surplus (i.e., leisure) time, properly used. Even in the early 1950s, he could write, "In our . . . Western world total labor has vanquished leisure. Unless we regain the art of silence and thought, the ability for [creative] non-activity, unless we substitute true leisure for our hectic amusements, we will destroy our culture—and ourselves." Strong words, to be sure, but he was probably onto something. John Gage, former chief scientist of Sun Microsystems, likes to quip that an astonishingly high percentage of important new discoveries, inventions, and creative works are made by people who don't have to go to meetings.

Another interesting data point is the popularity of the Waldorf School of the Peninsula in Los Altos, California, among the super-achieving parents of Silicon Valley. Guess what: Computers, cell phones, and iPads are strictly forbidden to these children of the tech elite, in favor of pens, pencils, and, yes, knitting needles. Maybe you recall a certain creative college dropout who taught himself calligraphy rather than computer programming, and took the time out to get in touch with his inner self before going on to set the world on fire. (His name, of course, was Steve Jobs.)

The Pause Principle, and corollaries such as the returning popularity of the Walden Pond, getting-away-from-it-all concept, speak to the intuitive receptivity of these ideas with most people. Nearly everyone is in agreement that the demands of modern life and the modern workplace are such that more reflective activities are squeezed out— and that this is not a good thing. Part of the reason behind the continuing resonance of our A.T. Kearney Global Business Policy Council CEO Retreat program is that the executives who attend find value, for one or two long weekends per year, in the chance to step off the merry-go-round and think about and learn about broad, far-reaching concepts and trends from different vantage points that they are simply denied the opportunity to focus on otherwise. Yet the fact that Thoreau wrote about this need to unplug and recharge over 160 years ago, and Pieper 60 years ago, tells us that the challenge of finding clear thought in a modern context, while perhaps accelerating from Thoreau to Pieper to now, is hardly new. So the question remains why, despite recognition of the need, has this problem remained with us and why have we been unable to do anything about it?

The types of big-picture, high-concept questions likely to be asked by a more broadly inclined thinker are far less reassuring than those offered by a precise, solutions-driven technical mind. When time is short and deadlines are tight, who wouldn't prefer a sharp-penciled answer to a broad-brushstroke question? Yet the overconfidence furnished by analytical certitude in a fluid and rapidly changing world can be disastrous. John S. Hammond, Ralph L. Keeney and Howard Raiffa, in their important 1998 *Harvard Business Review* piece "The Hidden Traps in Decision Making," would call this the Estimating and Forecasting Trap: overconfidence in a clear conception of the future that could be wrong, rather than planning around a more flexible view. This is not meant in any way to disparage the contributions that talented engineers and highly skilled technicians make to organizations, businesses, and governments, around the world. It is simply a plea for greater balance in the skills that we value both as business leaders and as a society. Today's world is too complex to manage without the technical abilities of engineers and scientists—but it is too unpredictable, and still too little understood not to incorporate the integrative perspectives of different thinking styles. Success requires the technical and the intuitive, as well as the pragmatic acknowledgement that we must act without waiting for that ever-elusive (and, in fact, never attained) certainty about every aspect of what we're doing or seeking.

Think Pinball, Not Roulette

As for the past few rollercoaster years, you wouldn't be human if you didn't also feel some sense of dread, given the relentless stream of changes, shocks, and crises affecting everything from your retirement nest egg to your children's career options. By dread, I mean the kind of apprehension that is nasty and visceral (right to the gut), and makes you feel like a bystander with little or no control over the forces shaping your life. Oscar Wilde said more than a century ago, "To expect the unexpected shows a thoroughly modern intellect," but he surely meant that as a bit of a joke. Since the sudden decompression of the world economy in 2007—no joke to us—analysts and pundits have been working (and talking) overtime to make sense of it all. Some blame too much leverage and easy credit, others too little regulation, and still others the proliferation of exotic financial instruments that few had heard of and even fewer understood. Some finger the role of terrorism and the trillion-dollar wars that it sparked, others the gravity-defying structural problems of the Eurozone. Many cite the excesses of the hype-driven, U.S.-centric "exaggeration economy" of recent years, where too many did the unforgivable: They actually came to believe their own press releases.

Respected economist Tyler Cowen, however, points to other, deeper patterns of change: In his view, by the turn of the twenty-first century, the United States had already gobbled up all the low-hanging fruit of growth—vast amounts of free land, a hundred million highly motivated immigrants, and the truly life-changing technological break-throughs of the twentieth century (from the telephone and TV to the automobile and jetliner), leaving America's increasingly mature growth engine sputtering. He has an interesting point, to be sure. Not a few opinion-makers have described the global economy as having become a vast casino by the mid-2000s, with the house (i.e., Wall Street and its counterparts elsewhere) getting ever more effective at picking inves-tors' pockets—and leaving the mess for others to clean up.

Still another view might be called reverting to type. This under-standing of history sees the world simply returning to norms that were briefly (by historical standards) interrupted by the Industrial Revolu-tion and the ascendancy of the West. Proponents of this perspective will point out that China was the world's largest economy and Asia the center of global economic activity for thousands of years. Driven by advances in technology, military organization, jurisprudence, and other "killer apps" (as called by Scottish-born Harvard academic Niall Ferguson), Europe and its overseas footholds reversed this status quo strongly in their favor. But how much longer can this Western leader-ship role last given certain demographic fundamentals and the universal availability of technological advances? How long could it have remained the case that two-thirds of all economic activity took place in areas where only one-tenth of all the world's population lived? Those taking this position see the decline of the West, at least in relative terms, as absolutely inevitable.

There is the additional notion that the globalization that led to the preeminence of the Western powers was inherently unstable, driven by the creation of ephemeral wealth over enduring value. As Mark Carney, governor of the Bank of Canada (Canada's central bank) said during the aftermath of the recent world financial crisis: "The next wave of globalization needs to be more firmly grounded and its participants more responsible. In recent years, a belief in the power of markets has not always been accompanied by a commitment to build resilient markets. Moreover, at times, policy-makers and the private sector did not live up to their responsibilities."

Which one of these interpretations is right? Actually, they all are—each has an element of truth that should be carefully weighed and considered in light of other views. The trouble, however, with oversubscribing to a single perspective or analysis is that each of these, by their very nature, is based on only a single (or at best a limited few) truths or insights. Focusing too exclusively on any one line of reasoning leaves you exposed to the false negative of unconsidered possibilities. So each interpretation can be (partially) correct and informative, but equally misleading if swallowed whole.

To go back to those who feel the world has become a vast roulette table, I say this: A better metaphor for our world is a pinball machine, and to understand that I might suggest a trip up the Old Santa Fe Trail, to the renowned Santa Fe Institute (SFI), home to Nobel laureates and a pioneer in the emerging field of complex systems. SFI's mouthful of a definition is "systems that display unpredictable . . . behavior result-ing from the interactions between their components. They are characterized by interconnectedness, feedback processes, non–linear change and tipping points, and emergent properties at the macro–level that cannot be predicted by understanding the component parts." While this doesn't exactly roll off the tongue, it's a profoundly impor-tant concept with powerful real-life applications, as we'll see.

Just as some thinkers believe history is shaped by great individuals, or by climate change, or by technology, or by new ideas, the reality is closer to a complex pinball-like interaction of all of these and more. Events, ideas (good and bad), great leaders (and tyrants), weather, new innovations, individual choices, natural disasters, wars, migrations, sheer accidents, and many other driving forces ricochet off each other—and now faster than ever before.

What's an example? Well, in centuries past, events in a small, remote country would not really reverberate anywhere else—it was a bit like the sound of a tree falling in an empty forest, to use that old expression. Fast-forward to our time, and events in a small, remote country called Iceland shook the world recently—twice over. Iceland's financial collapse not only made world markets shudder and caused big losses in many other places, but the volcanic island country's 2010 eruption caused the biggest air traffic shutdown since World War II: 107,000 European flights were canceled, and some 5 million passengers were stranded. Tranquil Indian Ocean resorts in places like Mauritius, the Sey-chelles, and the Maldives were stunned because they are overwhelmingly depen-dent on the European airlift. Woody Wade, hotel industry futurist and former senior staff member of the famous Swiss hotel school in Lausanne, asks, "Could a volcanic eruption in Iceland cause a hotel to go bust in the Seychelles?" Had the ash cloud lasted a few more days, the answer to his question would likely have been "yes"!

> *Just as some thinkers believe history is shaped by great individuals, or by climate change, or by technology, or by new ideas, the reality is closer to a complex pinball-like interaction of all of these and more.*

The truly bad news is that as systems become more complex (and as speed helps crank up complexity), they become more vulnerable, and our economic and political systems are now exceedingly so. As SFI notes, "At this point, we have a veritable zoo of systemic failures— failures in functioning, failures in design, and, certainly, failures in understanding. The list could be extended, too easily, to include the perceptual exaggerations induced by communications media, increasing economic dependence on the Internet, and the struggles for control mediated by policy-making institutions."

No wonder everyone's feeling more than a bit discombobulated.

Disorientation and Decision Analysis

Faced with too much information and not enough understanding, people and organizations begin to grasp at fleeting pieces of certainty and take actions that make sense in such a context. The colloquialism "hindsight is always 20/20" is used to justify those decisions that fail, with the excuse being that only the perfect foresight gained from actually experiencing the future could have delivered sufficient information and insight. But the trouble is that, by perceiving the future and the world as inherently unknowable, we too often end up with, to paraphrase the quip about the Vietnam War, one logical decision after another that when put together spell disaster.

So what are the most common reactions to information overload and confused perception? I submit that there are four:

• When faced with a complex, confusing, and constantly changing world, people and organizations freeze and take no action. One of the more gripping images illustrating this behavior is the reaction of George W. Bush when informed of the September 11, 2001, terrorist attacks. Reportedly for a solid seven minutes he was transfixed by an event the ramifications of which were simply beyond immediate comprehension. (Bush, of course, did ultimately take fairly dramatic action—but some would argue that this action was subject to the failings of point number three, below.) The shortcomings here are obvious—freezing and delaying yields missed opportunities for purposeful action, and erodes competitive advantage.

- When presented with massive complexity, people and organizations begin a process of analyzing and categorizing what they see in an attempt to get a handle on the situation and make thorough, data-driven decisions. There's hardly a consultant in existence who would discount the value of thorough analysis, and I'm not about to buck that trend. In fact, a good part of the success of my firm over its 85-plus year history has been based on its rigorous and exhaustive fact-based analyses. However, too frequently one can fall victim to what the executive coaches at Hogan Assessment Systems call "living in the weeds, excessive ideation, or dwelling on the why"—that is, focusing excessively on details at the expense of the bigger picture, with inaction or action made ineffective by delaying the inevitable result.

- The third reaction is a commonly applied antidote to the second— we begin to overanalyze, but in order to avoid inaction, we actually short-circuit the process and reach a single conclusion that, due to our faith in the analysis conducted, is viewed as immutable.

- Finally, and most commonly, information overload leads to frenetic, unfocused activity, devoid of clarity or purpose—like deciding to work on e-mail for hours in order to avoid more thorny problems at hand.

Information overload is a contributing factor that has made decision paralysis both more visible and more dangerous: more visible because it has become nearly ubiquitous and more dangerous because it exists in a more complex, and therefore more vulnerable, environment. The root cause, however, is not merely the volume of information or the heightened complexity of the modern business environment. Rather, it includes the rigid thinking styles and the lack of peripheral vision that we apply to these situations.

Chapter 2

Fast and Fickle

The Ever-Shorter Half-Life of Everything

It's not the speed that kills you, but the sudden stop.
—Rüdiger Dornbusch,
late MIT economist

Global capital markets pose the same kinds of problems that jet planes do. They are faster, more comfortable, and they get you where you are going better. But the crashes are much more spectacular.
—Larry Summers, twenty-seventh President of Harvard University and former U.S. Secretary of the Treasury

The gleaming new Lehman Brothers Europe headquarters in London opened in 2004, and in 2010 auction house Christie's sold two signs from there for £70,800 as souvenirs from the financial wreckage. As a Christie's executive said, "The attraction lies in the car-crash element."
SOURCE: Thomson Reuters.

It's hard to believe now, but in the early twentieth century, a number of artistic movements regarded speed, noise, motion, machines, crowds, and even industrial pollution as thrilling and liberating—the Italian Futurists, the British Vorticists, the American designers of sleek, streamlined locomotives and gleaming propeller aircraft. (Tiffany still sells a line of jewelry called Streamerica based on the aesthetics of speed from the time when ocean liners where breaking Transatlantic records.)

In our own time, we find velocity more unsettling—and destabilizing. For example, in the blink of an eye, Finnish mobile phone giant Nokia has gone from being the darling of the business world to a company teetering on the edge of an abyss. Stephen Elop, Nokia's newly appointed CEO, has written about the company being a burning platform—a striking image in the wake of the BP Gulf of Mexico disaster. Elop's message to employees (that was duly leaked to the press) described an overly slow and insular corporate culture, one that was simultaneously unable to see over the horizon or to successfully tack with the wind. As a result, Nokia was a late entrant to the smartphone wars (a segment now dominated by Apple, which was not in the mobile phone business five years ago, and Samsung, which had previously been known for low-cost, standard mobile devices). When Nokia did arrive on the scene it was unable to keep up with the advances of its competitors.

While we don't yet fully understand all of the internal dynamics that led to Nokia's decline (although I'm sure it won't be long before some clever researcher writes up a case on it for B-school types to study in future years), it seems likely that they fell victim to at least some of what John S. Hammond, Ralph L. Keeney, and Howard Raiffa termed Decision Traps in their seminal *Harvard Business Review* article

The average lifespan of a Fortune 500 company used to be about 40 to 50 years according to onetime Shell scenario planner Arie de Geus. But Peter Senge of MIT estimates that this number is now closer to 30 years.

referenced earlier. These heuristic flaws, they write, are "well-documented psychological traps that are particularly likely to undermine business decisions." In the context of Nokia, there are two in particular that come to mind: the Sunk Cost Trap, which involves redoubling your efforts because of investments to date, and the Confirming Evidence Trap, in which organizations seek out only that evidence that supports the prevailing point of view.

We have no choice but to get used to it: The accelerating pace of change and the fickleness of consumer tastes mean that the half-life of any company, product, brand, or great idea is a lot shorter than it used to be. Add to that the challenge of facing increased competition in a globalized marketplace, corporate governance structures that all too frequently incentivize overly risky (or overly cautious) behaviors, and it's easy to see why so many iconic corporations have either disappeared or have become unrecognizable. The average lifespan of a Fortune 500 company used to be about 40 to 50 years according to onetime Shell scenario planner Arie de Geus. But Peter Senge of MIT estimates that this number is now closer to 30 years. Author Jim Collins, of *Built-to-Last* fame, notes that of the original 500 companies on the 1955 list, just 71 are in existence today. As the global economy becomes an increasingly complex—and therefore fragile—system, the companies that operate within it have become increasingly complex and vulnerable in tandem. Individuals can be left feeling bewildered, while companies can find themselves continually on the defensive, searching for a strategic foothold in a landscape that is constantly changing.

The late Peter Drucker, as always, seemed to get it before everybody else (writing here in the September 1994 edition of *Harvard Business Review*):

The root cause of nearly every business crisis is not that things are being done poorly. It is not even that the wrong things are being done. . . . But rather because the assumptions on which the organization has been built and is being run no longer fit reality. These are assumptions that shape any organization's behavior, dictate its decisions about what to do, and define what the organization considers meaningful results. These are assumptions about markets. They are about identifying customers and competitors, their values and behaviors. They are about technology and its dynamics, about a company's strengths and weaknesses, about what a company gets paid for, a company's theory of business.

> *The root cause of nearly every business crisis is not that things are being done poorly. It is not even that the wrong things are being done. . . . But rather because the assumptions on which the organization has been built and is being run no longer fit reality.*
>
> —*Peter Drucker*

In short, consumers, companies, and governments clinging to outmoded concepts of product, business, and idea cycles will be left continually flat-footed. Compare for a moment the disparate fortunes of General Motors and Volkswagen. Much has been made of the difficult structural environment that GM operated in, with high labor costs and massive pension and healthcare obligations. But it would be difficult to say that a German company does not face at least similar challenges. Yet GM went bankrupt, saved only by the *deus ex machina* of the United States and Canadian governments, and even now is only just returning to profitability. Volkswagen, by contrast, is both a larger vehicle maker than GM (by some measures—VW sold 8.4 million vehicles in 2011 versus 9 million for GM, but some analysts observe that GM's number is inflated by fleet sales) and a hugely profitable one to boot, with 2011 profits reaching an all-time high of 11.3 billion euros. Some of this is due to transition costs as GM moves away from a product portfolio skewed toward gas-guzzling SUVs and pickups and belatedly rationalizes a needlessly large and incoherent stable of brands (although it must be noted that VW has been successful at marketing a number of overlapping marques). However, more had to do with GM's structural rigidity and bloated internal processes. Even now, four years after its bankruptcy, GM is producing vehicles on 30 different platforms (the intensely expensive to develop architecture that is the underpinning of a particular vehicle), with a goal of reducing this number to 14 by 2018. With the launch of its MQB (Modularer Querbaukasten) platform in the Audi A3, VW will produce the majority of its vehicles on just four.

Lumbering Giants

> If you don't like change, you're going to like irrelevance even less.
>
> —U.S. General Eric "Rick" Shinseki

As institutions structurally geared to be slow moving, governments may face the greatest challenge—particularly those seeking to balance short-term fiscal pressures with long-term competitiveness and entitlements challenges. Time and again, the situation is aggravated by data paralysis and rigid organizational thinking. Successful governments, companies, and individuals need to defy the laws of gravity and both think and act longer-term and cross-border—and quickly. Enlightened policy decisions all too often promise benefits that are long term and diffuse, while delivering immediate, palpable pain that affects clearly identified constituencies: hardly a compelling political proposition.

Speaking of shorter half-lives, have you noticed the way the acronym BRICs (for Brazil, Russia, India, China) has gone from ubiquity to near-obsolescence in just a few years? People and organizations need to accept paradigms in order to be able to take action, and the BRICs idea provided useful shorthand for thinking about opportunities in the big emerging markets. The case of the BRICs paradigm makes this complex mix abundantly clear: Yes, the locus of economic dynamism, brainpower, and even military force is shifting fast from West to East and from North to South. The problem is that the exact implications are hard to gauge. China's ambitions, for example, go well beyond economic growth and commercial success, as its building of a potent, blue-water navy that may soon rival the U.S. Seventh Fleet in the Pacific shows. In response, America is launching the most expensive weapons system ever developed: the Gerald R. Ford class of nuclear-powered super-carriers, each one "100,000 tons and 4.5 acres of mobile and sovereign U.S. territory," according to the Navy's own promotional language. The United States and China depend vitally on one another's economies, but superpower aspirations and frictions may at some point trump economic and trade considerations, as these massive military investments suggest.

So will the twenty-first century be more peaceful than the last one? We sure hope so, but we just don't know. We do know that emerging markets, big and small, are no longer just low-cost manufacturing hubs. They are high-end consumer markets in their own right as well as very sophisticated investors (not borrowers) in the United States and Europe. As one finds in Washington, D.C., the great megacities of the emerging world have enclaves of extraordinary wealth sitting near pockets of desperate poverty. In fact, places like Lagos, Nigeria (where I spent time early on in my career), are literal time machines: You can go from the twenty-first century to the Stone Age just by crossing the street.

The striking thing, however, about the less privileged sections of Lagos, or São Paulo, or Mumbai, is the ubiquitous presence of advanced technology juxtaposed with living conditions that could be considered barely medieval. Seemingly everyone in the Stone Age section of these megacities will still have a mobile phone. Mobile phone penetration in the developing world is strikingly high—Brazil's mobile penetration rate, for example, was 114 percent at the end of 2011, with 28 million more mobile subscribers than people, and India alone has over 880 million wireless subscribers. And the technology available is rapidly moving from 2G, or voice-only, service to 3G standards, long available in the developed world, that support mobile Internet connectivity as well—with a number of surprising benefits. For example, on one of my recent trips to India, I learned that increased access to 3G mobile phones by migrant workers has been credited with a reduction in that demographic group's consumption of alcohol. Rather than drinking (sometimes excessively) as a principal recreational activity after a hard day, workers can divert themselves instead by streaming cricket matches or the latest Bollywood film to their handheld devices. Expect trends like this to accelerate as next-generation, superfast 4G wireless technology is rolled out in India over the coming years, led by Reliance Industries' visionary leader Mukesh Ambani (author of this book's foreword). Media reports are that Reliance plans to offer 4G data services at just 10 rupees (US$0.20) per gigabyte—one-tenth the current price of the nearest competitor.

The introduction of new consumer technologies can have interesting and unforeseen consequences. Some have linked the widespread adoption of television in the United States, which went from a virtual zero in 1950 to 86.9 percent in 1960 and to 95.3 percent in 1970, to lower birthrates, which fell 25 percent over the same period. The insinuation being that as televisions became more and more a part of daily lives and entertainment, people engaged less frequently in more traditional (and procreative) activities. Of course, the broad acceptance of contraception over the same period was clearly a contributing factor as well, but it will be interesting to see what the ripple effects of mobile infotainment are in some of the world's rapidly developing economies.

More generally, as I look around the emerging world, I see surprises. Take Brazil, which for decades was a chronically inflation-ridden, chaotic underperformer. It now is the world's most productive and efficient agribusiness powerhouse. And the handsome regional jet you're catching tonight in the United States or Western Europe may well have been skillfully designed and built in São José dos Campos, Brazil, by Embraer, and sold for a very attractive price. Many think Mexico and think urban drug wars . . . but how many realize that the loaf of bread they're buying in a supermarket is now produced by Mexico's world-class Bimbo Group—the world's largest baker?

And, more often than not, success is fleeting: just take a quick stroll down memory lane by looking at such iconic business books as *Good* to *Great* and *In Search of Excellence.* There you'll find case studies on such paragons of innovation as Fannie Mae, Amdahl, Data General, Digital Equipment, Wang Labs, and many others that will surprise you, in hindsight. Of course, in their day, these were great companies, and any ranking of innovators is inevitably a snapshot of a moving target. Another important aspect is that adversity can be a great teacher, and some of the most tenacious innovators were literally born in hard times (for example, the founding of FedEx, Microsoft, and Apple in the stagflation 1970s).

Even further back we see that powerhouses such as General Electric (founded in 1892) and Procter & Gamble (founded in 1837) were established or came of age during the so-called Long Depression—a period of prolonged stagnation that ran from 1873 to 1893. This now largely forgotten era began with a financial crisis

Take Brazil, which for decades was a chronically inflation-ridden, chaotic underperformer. It now is the world's most productive and efficient agribusiness powerhouse. And the handsome regional jet you're catching tonight in the United States or Western Europe may well have been skillfully designed and built in São José dos Campos, Brazil, by Embraer, and sold for a very attractive price.

driven by railroad speculation that triggered a six-year recession that was followed by a decade-and-a-half of meager growth and high unemployment. If that scenario sounds uncomfortably similar to the global economic situation now, you wouldn't be the first to think so. The question to ask, however, is not how long the present malaise will last, but which of today's companies are taking advantage of hard-to-see opportunities to lay the foundation for sustained future growth?

But if you're not looking for innovative ideas or opportunities, or are unprepared to react to a discovery once made, you're not going to find yourself in a position to innovate or succeed. You can't spend all your time reacting to the fast and fickle of global change. To be sure, you need to have enough operational acumen to allow your organization to survive to reach its future potential, but you have to maintain a view of the longer term to help seize that future. This is as true for individual career or investment decisions as much as it is if you are leading a business or making government policy decisions. You might say you need a foot on the brake and a foot on the gas pedal.

Consider two of the examples of successful companies that I mentioned earlier in this chapter, Apple and Volkswagen. Each one has been driven by a strong sense of strategic direction that has not wavered with the news or business cycle. There are many reasons for this, but central consideration should be paid to the leadership and organizational models that these two companies have followed.

In the case of Apple, the company's success was driven over a sustained period by the vision and perfectionist focus of its late CEO, Steve Jobs. Impervious to media or analyst criticism—he even declined to provide earnings forecasts to investors—Jobs had the courage of his convictions and revolutionized not just the consumer electronics industry, but the media, music, and entertainment industries as well. It seems unlikely that this success could be replicated by an executive who swayed with the wind and responded to each and every fleeting consumer trend.

Volkswagen has the long view organizationally embedded in its corporate structure. Like most German public companies, its supervisory board consists not only of management and shareholder representatives, but union leaders and government officials as well. While this can make corporate governance even more complicated, it does broaden the scope of corporate interests to include the views of stakeholders whose motivations extend beyond quarterly earnings reports—and helps to moderate and smooth corporate decisions. And while it is one of the world's largest automakers, VW is in many ways a family company. It was founded in 1937 by Ferdinand Porsche, the designer of the iconic VW Beetle (for, embarrassingly, Adolf Hitler), and its main shareholders today are his descendants, including his grandson, Ferdinand Piëch, VW's chairman. While Piëch does not garner the same media attention as a Steve Jobs (or even a Steve Ballmer), he is every bit the automotive visionary and an obsessive car guy with a keen sense of the long-term and his legacy. In fact, reports are that he has constructed a trust for his shares to help ensure his 12 children, when they inherit them, do not divest them outside of the family.

I remember hearing British management thinker Charles Handy say in the late 1990s that companies ought to have two classes of shareholders: a permanent class of voting shareholders who cannot sell their shares except at specified times and a second class of nonvoting shareholders who can trade in and out as often as they would like (punters, as Charles called them). Although this is a not a new idea (many family-controlled, publicly traded companies in Europe have dual-class share structures), it's interesting to note that this kind of idea resonates strongly in Silicon Valley. With Google's recent share split, the newly issued shares will be nonvoting, allowing the founders to retain their long-term control. Some corporate governance experts and institutional investors are horrified, but other investors see such control as something resembling long-term stewardship.

Antonio Borges, the corporate governance expert who has had a particularly illustrious career as head of IMF Europe, vice chairman of Goldman Sachs International, dean of the highly-regarded INSEAD business school, and deputy governor of the Portuguese central bank, likes to show the contrast between U.S., British, and continental European governance models—with important lessons for all parts of the world.

In Antonio's view, the U.S. system has traditionally had the lowest corporate governance standards (at least until the recent avalanche of legislation and regulation), with little distinction between management and directors and widespread use of poison pills, staggered boards, and non-independent directors, including CEOs who are also simultaneously board chairmen. The saving grace of the U.S. system has always been the primacy of the market—with underperformers getting swift payback from the market, including management firings and takeovers. The central problem has always been the temptation to deceive the market, as we saw with Enron and many other cases we would now rather forget.

The UK has typically been viewed as having the most advanced governance standards, at least on paper. In comparison with the United

States, the market is less powerful, less decisive—but British executives feel under pressure from their boards, and very much accountable to them. The clear role of management is running the company, and the clear business of the directors is governance—the players and the coaches, if you will.

In continental Europe, founder-owners and family shareholders tend to control many listed (publicly-traded) companies, and this is not necessarily an inferior model: They demand good performance and high standards. The problem with this system is how to guarantee the running of the company in the interests of all the shareholders, not merely those with a controlling stake.

Might it be best to bring together the best aspects of all three systems, combining rigorous market discipline, director independence (including strict separation of powers), and active ownership to corporations everywhere? Hanging over these issues is the seeming paradox of the many companies that have combined excellent performance with poor governance (and vice versa) over the years.

Some will point out that the models pursued by companies I've mentioned in this chapter have clear drawbacks. Centering corporate identity on a singular cult of personality embodied in the chief executive (as many claim was the case with Apple) can expose such an organization to considerable risks in the event of the passing or departure of such a key figure. Time will tell if this is the case with Apple, but early indications are that Jobs, with a strong sense of his own mortality, left behind a cadre of talented executives imbued with a determination similar to his own (albeit with perhaps less flair). Similarly, the record of family companies over multiple generations is mixed, with later generations often lacking the passion or talent of their forebears. However, for an example in successful transition, Piëch has only to look south to Fiat, where controlling shareholder and Italian icon Gianni Agnelli handpicked a very able successor in his grandson, John Elkann, to serve as chairman of both Fiat and Exor, the Agnelli family investment vehicle with holdings as diverse as Fiat, Cushman & Wakefield, and the Juventus football club. (Elkann, in turn, had the wisdom to select Sergio Marchionne to turn around Fiat, which is now looking more robust than it has in decades.)

Speaking for my own organization, I can say this: At A.T. Kearney, looking beyond the fast and fickle has been an intense focus—especially during our post–MBO (Management Buy-Out) resurgence over the past six years. Since our beginning, our corporate culture and consulting style have been based on driving improved operational performance and not just offering advice. (We've tried to capture the spirit of this in our new brand statement of "Immediate Impact, Growing Advantage.")

Watch Out for Those Tuning Out and Checking Out

Things aren't what they used to be, and probably never were.
—Will Rogers

I don't want to get too nostalgic for earlier Golden Ages that never really existed, but we used to have much more of a common culture than we have today. In part this was due to a limited number of choices (I can recall growing up with just three television channels!), forcing everybody to watch the same evening newscasts and read *Time* or *LIFE* (or the equivalent in other countries). Similarly, without the technological enablement (and imperilment) that we face today, the pace of life was slower and people had the time to engage in more face-to-face contact, and to participate in local city and community institutions. While there were clear drawbacks to the less technologi- cally advanced life, an important consequence of limited options meant that people had to engage with and accommodate neighbors and fellow citizens who had other personal interests and different political and religious views.

Today, by contrast, you can completely tune out of your local reality and absorb yourself in one or two narrow interests you pursue exclusively by way of your broadband connection and the security of your private cocoon. Sophisticated marketers are increasingly adept at using social networking tools to segment small groups into extreme versions of Edmund Burke's "little platoons"—but without the broader societal connectivity that he postulated. Burke wrote, "To be attached to the subdivision, to love the little platoon we belong to in society, is the first principle (the germ as it were) of public affections."

In a certain sense the modern process of psychographic segmentation is a natural extension of this idea. In psychographic segmentation, data on groups is taken beyond the standard measures of demographics, geography, or income, to encompass characteristics such as lifestyle, personality, social class, and AIO (an acronym for Attitudes, Interests, and Opinions) to understand potential influences on purchasing behavior. More recently, companies with significant amounts of data and powerful processors have developed psychographic algorithms that can be used to predict and encourage buying decisions, as Google does by displaying advertisements of potentially attractive products based on your Internet surfing history.

While it's very convenient to have Google constantly suggest to you products that are related to your recent purchases, or news topics that are somehow linked to your last few searches, there is also something strikingly limiting in this constant narrowing of circles. An even newer development is to have products pushed at you that have been purchased or highly rated by friends or role models in your social network, encouraging you and your associates to purchase goods that appeal to you and your peers, reinforced by receipt of the same news and opinions.

Isn't it rather ironic that the development of social networking, a technology originally designed to increase personal connectivity and broaden experiences and inputs, could ultimately end up reducing both? The problem is not the technology itself, or the ability to reach broader groups, but that the application has been to increase connections, often at the expense of relationships. A friend on Facebook or a connection on LinkedIn can be a net positive, and I'm not advocating against either, but these transactional links are too often viewed as substitutes for real relationships based on shared experience and mutual values.

I remember hearing Facebook COO Sheryl Sandberg in Davos assert that social networking opens up new possibilities for those reaching beyond their normal constrained personal networks to engage their electronic friends of friends, in Facebook parlance. She recounts, for example, how couples who have been unable to adopt a child through normal channels report having had their dreams fulfilled by extending their reach to a larger, electronically enabled group of friends who share enough interest and affinity to help. Picture the headline: Friends of Friends Helped Us Adopt Our Child.

But again, for many people, the accumulation of connections bears little resemblance to the development of true relationships. And this is in no way limited to the personal realm—in fact businesses may be the greater offenders. One has only to look at the cultural evolution within investment bank Goldman Sachs during its period of breakneck growth. An institution once known for its collegial team culture and overriding emphasis on long-term client relationships has been criticized as an increasingly transaction-minded firm by a prominent departing senior executive. Some employees derisively called their clients muppets—as the world came to know from Greg Smith's now-famous op-ed piece in the *New York Times* headlined "Why I Am Leaving Goldman Sachs."

On that note, sometimes an opulent new headquarters signals a shift in corporate culture, or even a peak: Goldman, which was previously content to base itself in an unexceptional precast concrete office tower in lower Manhattan's Broad Street for decades, moved, in 2009, to a purpose-built new head office designed by star architects Pei Cobb Freed at 200 West Street. According to architectural critic Paul Goldberger, it's a sleek, 43-story "understated palazzo." Whether it will ultimately be seen as an iconic headquarters symbolizing the strength and creativity of the firm that built it, or as a white elephant conceived and planned during the tail end of the 2000s boom, we'll have to wait and see. At the time of this writing, Facebook has officially settled into its headquarters campus in Menlo Park, California, with the address of 1 Hacker Way. It's also worth taking a look at, if only to catch a whiff of Silicon Valley success circa 2012.

As for the long and the short of it, these developments don't exactly make for an engaged or aligned citizenry either, to say the least. The enclave communities that result are increasingly apparent even in melting-pot societies, where technology allows new waves of immigrants to avoid assimilation by permitting low-cost, instantaneous connection to one's country of origin. When I was a child growing up in a New York City teeming with new immigrants, my immigrant Italian father and first-generation mother had no prospect of returning home on low-cost air carriers, or calling home to stay connected to the old world, or even to turn on Italian-language TV. One had no choice but to assimilate and strive to become—in so many cases—more American than apple pie.

It also doesn't help that in the sphere of education, outcomes are increasingly bipolar: from the best of the best at America's great research universities, Britain's "Oxbridge," and a subset of well-funded private and suburban schools around the world—to the worsening conditions nearly everywhere else. Under-education goes hand-in-hand with under- or unemployment (and despair), and functional illiteracy is so common that we hardly notice it anymore. Even at the level of the elite, the phenomenon of ever-narrower specialization means that the emerging generation of managers and technologists may not have enough broad knowledge to have the peripheral vision that real leaders need. When college and business school students (and my children) ask me what they should do, I tell them to follow their passions and develop expertise in some field, while becoming lifelong learners and keeping tuned in to a broader horizon. Deep domain knowledge, while necessary, just isn't enough anymore to propel career success on its own, no more than it is a sufficiently alert business model.

Given all this complexity cubed, you can see why retreating to your own private cocoon may be appealing to many today (if they can afford it). Some well-heeled folks want to check out even further: A group of young, mostly Silicon Valley tycoons are funding the Seasteading Movement, which wants to experiment with new private jurisdictions that are literally offshore platforms outside of territorial waters. I suppose you can't completely blame them, given the sense of disconnect many people feel from politics and the lack of confidence they have in their governments or the next generation of leaders. A more modest concept being funded by

Given all this complexity cubed, you can see why retreating to your own private cocoon may be appealing to many today (if they can afford it).

some seasteading investors is Blueseed, "Silicon Valley's visa-free off-shore community." With a planned launch in late 2013 or early 2014, Blueseed will offer tech people from around the world a place to live and work on a ship anchored 12 miles off the Bay Area coast, in international waters. As the promoters say, no need to mess with complicated U.S. H1-B visas and the like anymore. Your Silicon Valley (and American) dream awaits on this "Googleplex of the sea."

In the meantime, would-be seasteaders can buy an apartment on the MS *The World*, "the only private residential community-at-sea where its residents may travel the world without ever leaving home." Operated by ResidenSea of Miramar, Florida, the ship flies a Bahamian flag and has about 165 studios and suites ranging in price from $600K to around $13 million. Monthly maintenance fees start at about $20,000 and go up from there. According to media reports quoting some unhappy owners, despite its glamorous itinerary sailing from Cape Town to Polynesia and then over to Rio for Carnival and so forth, the atmosphere onboard reportedly isn't always blissful, and then there are the annoying additional paying guests the ship has been taking on for a tiny fraction of what the apartment owners pay. Utopia has never been so elusive.

You don't have to think very long or hard to understand why escapism (in all its forms) appeals so much these days. Perhaps you yourself bought a copy of the wildly successful (and amusing) book *The 4-Hour Workweek* by Timothy Ferriss, which describes a very hard-to-duplicate model of how to outsource your life and career for fun and profit. Reporters have noted that Ferriss has even sub-contracted his romantic life "by asking digital assistants to find dates for him." A. J. Jacobs, an editor of *Esquire* magazine, quipped that the team he hired in India to plan a party, read his e-mails, and answer his phone was so successful that he "even paid one to take responsibility for his anxieties." According to Jacobs, presumably writing slightly tongue-in-cheek, "The outsourcing of my neuroses was one of my most successful experiments. . . . Every time I started to ruminate, I'd remind myself that [the remote digital assistant] was already on the case and I'd relax."

On the flip side, younger people with fewer means are checking out in their own way by rejecting, in increasing numbers, the conventional

notion of adulthood altogether. Parents who used to view their obligations to their offspring as financial commitments lasting 22 or 24 years,
now realize that their children may be dependents well into their 30s
or even 40s. A recent report by the Pew Research Center found that
29 percent of U.S. adults ages 25 to 34 live with their parents—this
group has been dubbed the boomerang generation. Rather than being
concerned about any social stigma associated with this, as there may
have been for GenX-ers of previous years, 78 percent of boomerang
children are satisfied with this arrangement, and just 25 percent
reported additional strain on their relationship with their parents. The
United States is hardly alone in this trend: in France 31 percent of the
25-to-34 age group live with their parents, in Germany about 40
percent, and in Great Britain the figure is almost 42 percent. In Spain,
hard hit by a burst housing bubble and with youth unemployment
over 50 percent, a whopping 52.2 percent of the 25-to-34-year-old
group live with parents.

Part of this, of course, has to do with the continuing economic
weakness and bleak entry-level job prospects, and the economic need
may not only be manifest with the boomerangers. In fact, Pew found
that 89 percent of boomerang children assist with household expenses
and a full 48 percent pay rent to their parents. But beyond all this,
many young people appear to be reluctant to take the leap into independent life, and for some there is even a notion that the world as
presently constituted is not worth accepting. The *Washington City
Paper*—not necessarily the most prestigious journalistic presence, but
frequently a very good leading indicator—recently ran a headline
reading: "Against Adulthood: I Don't Wanna Grow Up!" In an age of
crisis, nothing looks quite so unappealing—or elusive—as the prospect
of settling down in an unsettled world.

Chapter 3

Rudderless World

Angry Populism, Incapacitated Government,
and Stray Capitalism

We all know what to do, but we don't know how to get re-elected once we have done it.
> —Jean-Claude Juncker, Prime Minister of Luxembourg
> and former President of the European Council

The working of great institutions is mainly the result of a vast mass of routine, petty malice, self-interest, carelessness, and sheer mistake. Only a residual fraction is thought.
> —George Santayana, Spanish-born thinker
> and Harvard professor

The natural state of men, before they were joined in society, was a war, and not simply, but a war of all against all.
> —Thomas Hobbes

To paraphrase the Beatles, you say you want a revolution? Well, today streets around the world are filled with enraged people, but unlike the 1960s protest movements, this rage doesn't seem to be leading to any particular destination.
SOURCE: Kevork Djansezian/Getty Images.

In Davos about 10 years ago, I caught the whiff of something reminiscent of my college days in the late 1960s in Chicago: tear gas. I was in the famous Swiss ski village for the World Economic Forum's annual confab, a place where you can indeed meet more CEOs and movers and shakers and pick up more new stimuli in several days than you can in a year of traveling. The country is justly famed for an orderliness bordering on the obsessive-compulsive, and for this annual event, the security is always wound as tightly as the spring on a handcrafted Swiss watch.

So amid the police patrols with machine pistols and Alsatian dogs, why was there a riot unfolding right before my eyes? This was not the storming of the Bastille, but rather the storming of the local McDonald's outlet in Davos. Initially, it didn't make sense to me: The mass protests I remembered from my days at the University of Chicago in the late 1960s had very concrete objectives (e.g., stop the Vietnam War, equal rights for African Americans or women, clean up the environment, and so on). But smashing Ronald McDonald? Seriously, what would that accomplish? (Sure, it was quite a publicity stunt and got headlines galore.)

Tea Party, Occupy Movements: Birds of a Feather?

I only later fully understood the importance of this event, which was not about a specific policy agenda or a pressure group's negotiating position. It was about *rage*. As we have learned the hard way, events anywhere now reverberate everywhere instantly. And, unsurprisingly,

As we have learned the hard way, events anywhere now reverberate everywhere instantly. And, unsurprisingly, large numbers of people find the pace of change frightening and confusing. Some grasp at bizarre conspiracy theories. Others gravitate to extremist groups or politics, unfortunately a still-rising trend.

large numbers of people find the pace of change frightening and confusing. Some grasp at bizarre conspiracy theories. Others gravitate to extremist groups or politics, unfortunately a still-rising trend. Populist movements like Occupy and the Tea Party are bubbling up around the world, even in normally quiet Scandinavia—where the anti-EU True Finns party has taken a key role in the Finnish parliament. A common thread binding these groups is the gut feeling that political institutions have been corrupted or co-opted, and that, short of a significant intervention, they are simply no longer responsive to the needs of ordinary citizens. These groups vary in the level of detachment felt from their governments: the True Finns use the institutions of their national government to protest a supranational structure (the EU), the Tea Party wishes to project change through government but has side-stepped the traditional party structures, and the Occupy movement exists outside of any recognizable organizational shape altogether.

None of their ideologies strike me as especially coherent, but it's difficult to deny the level of popular appeal they have—and it's actually easy to comprehend the frustrations of their supporters. After all, how much real, vigorous, public debate has truly gone into some of the most momentous political decisions in recent history? The euro and many other important EU developments came about without direct citizen participation—and no wonder, since the track record for pan-European measures making it through the ballot box is far from stellar. The Iraq War was largely a fait accompli, as was TARP, the auto bail-outs, and so many other recent—and controversial—political decisions. The point here is not about whether one agrees or disagrees with specific political actions, or even in some cases whether politicians were reasonably in a position to solicit public input prior to taking action in a crisis. It's no surprise that vast swaths of the public are feeling left out, mere bystanders to events not only beyond their control, but even beyond their ability to have the smallest say.

Lord (Chris) Patten, the last governor of Hong Kong, who is now chancellor of Oxford University and chairman of the BBC, puts it this way: Populism and protectionism come "in waves, let loose by insecurity, by fear of change, by xenophobia, by blindness to sometimes uncomfortable reality and yearnings for a golden age"—and are "as old as quack medicine, as immemorial as snake-oil salesmen and charlatan cures."

And not all of the public's primal fears are exaggerated or imaginary: There is nothing more scary than having your food or water supply tainted or interrupted, given natural disasters, changing weather patterns, supply disruptions, malicious activity, or other factors. Just look at the recent food riots on several continents and the wild swings in commodity prices. The anger that accompanies a sharp and seemingly arbitrary spike in the price of bread in some countries, by the way, is actually similar in intensity to the frustration that Tea Party members or True Finns feel about tax levels or EU regulations, only adjusted for different circumstances and levels of development.

Then again, some countries only flirt with populism, while for others, it has been a permanent scourge. Sebastian Edwards, Henry Ford II Professor at UCLA's Anderson School and former Latin American chief economist at the World Bank, says, "In 1700 the colonies of North and South America had roughly the same standard of living. By 1820, however, income per capita in Latin America was about two-thirds that of the U.S. and Canada. In 2009 Latin America's income per person was roughly one-fifth that of North America." Why? An endless, chaotic cycle of populist empty promises and misrule, basically. According to Sebastian, a brilliant Chilean and Chicago Boy (he has a doctorate from the University of Chicago), only Chile, of all the countries in the region, has ever managed to break this cycle—though he gives Brazil an honorable mention for the way in which its increasingly dynamic corporate sector has literally outgrown some of that vast country's historic problems. (Don't let the Welsh name

> *. . . Populist leaders exhibit an eloquent, charismatic and unlimited capacity to promise a better life for their people simply by wishing for it—never as the result of discipline, thrift and hard work. In practice the populists' expansionary policies have usually delivered short-lived prosperity. . . .*
> —*Ernesto Zedillo*

Edwards throw you off: Sebastian is a scion of one of Chile's great business dynasties, and in his spare time is a fine Spanish-language novelist to boot.)

Former Mexican President Ernesto Zedillo, now a professor at Yale (where he did graduate work in the 1970s), also speaks with some authority on this theme: "Whether authoritarian or democratic, rightist or leftist, populism has been the most pervasive political ideology in Latin American politics for nearly a century. . . . Populist leaders exhibit an eloquent, charismatic and unlimited capacity to promise a better life for their people simply by wishing for it—never as the result of discipline, thrift and hard work. In practice the populists' expansionary policies have usually delivered short-lived prosperity. This reality, coupled with the socially divisive rhetoric loved and employed by populists, has sometimes led to violence and opened the door to even worse authoritarian regimes." From the 1950s glamor of Evita and Juan Perón in Argentina, to the decades of Fidel Castro's tenure in Cuba, to the more recent power grab of Hugo Chávez in Venezuela, democratic trappings and slogans have frequently been a cover for strongman rule.

In fact, while the Peróns may be long dead, Peronism is very much alive, as we saw recently with Argentina's seizure and re-nationalization of the country's largest oil company, YPF—valued at around $10 billion—and until recently 51 percent owned by Spanish-based conglomerate Repsol. Moisés Naím, the Washington-based thinker and writer who was Venezuela's Minister of Trade and Industry during more reform-oriented days, says ". . . objective observers will agree that this was not part of an overarching development strategy, nor a manifestation of resource nationalism—nor indeed any other carefully crafted initiative forming part of a broader design. Rather cronyism, rifts between oligarchs, political expediency, populism, and the wish to please a public resentful of the privatizations of the 1990s all played into the decision."

Winston Churchill is reputed to have said, "Democracy is the worst form of government, except for all others." The democratic narrative has been largely ascendant, not just in the Western world but in developing countries alike for the past 200 years. Economist Daron Acemoglu of MIT and political scientist James Robinson of Harvard, in their book *Why Nations Fail: The Origins of Power, Prosperity, and Poverty*, trace the roots of what they call inclusive government further back, to England's so-called Glorious Revolution of 1688. Their thesis is that inclusive governments, or systems that are designed to allow equal political and economic engagement, foster growth, while extractive governments, typified by autocratic or authoritarian regimes, tend to concentrate wealth while simultaneously limiting growth and breeding instability. Inclusive, growth-creating governance has always been associated with democracy, but some have begun to question whether liberal representative systems indeed have a monopoly over broad-based growth and rising living standards.

In policy circles, the view that the key to economic development is a combination of democracy and open markets became known as the Washington Consensus, after the location of the International Monetary Fund (IMF), the World Bank, and the U.S. capital. While the Washington Consensus has its many critics (and proponents), the truly remarkable performance of China over the past 10-plus years has led to discussion about a "Beijing Consensus," in which limited freedoms coupled with managed openness apparently deliver even better economic returns. Is the Beijing Consensus ready to provide a counterpoint to Churchill's axiom? Few would bet on it at this point (China, of course, has its own set of issues, ranging from demographic transition to environmental degradation), but the level of dissatisfaction shown by groups living under the Washington Consensus at least makes this a compelling discussion.

Privatizing the Gains, Socializing the Losses

. . . We have promoted an insider form of capitalism which exploits and indeed creates subsidies and tax loopholes on which the insiders prosper [who have] rigged the game rather than won in honest competition.

—Martin Wolf, Chief Economics Commentator,
Financial Times

You can't prevent institutions from failing. I mean, it will happen, inevitably. It has to be that when an institution fails that it's borne by the shareholders, then their debt-holders, but not ultimately the taxpayer.

—Mark Carney, Governor of the Bank of Canada

One of the greatest engines of growth of all time was the development of the limited liability joint-stock company of the 1700s. It allowed investors to provide their capital in exchange for a share of the profits. What made this revolutionary was the fact that shareowners were neither stuck permanently, nor were their potential losses unlimited. They could trade out of their holdings, and their downside was limited to their initial investment. However, the losses were the responsibility of the company, not of the government or of society more broadly. This risk–reward structure is literally the foundation of the modern economy.

Bad news, folks: The model has broken down and we're feeling the pinch. The old joke about communism was that the government scooped up the goodies but socialized the losses—not exactly a motivating combination. Today, we have ended up in a similar place but with a capitalist twist: The losses are still borne by the public, but rather than a small group of commissars skimming the cream, that privilege is held by the well-connected and super-wealthy (dubbed with great effect by the various Occupy movements as "The 1 Percent"). Big-league investors, companies, hedge funds, bankers, public-sector borrowers, and so on often get to keep the winnings, while the losses (if big enough) are socialized by society at large.

Lest we think this is an entirely twenty-first century phenomenon, I offer the following quote from the United States' seventh president, Andrew Jackson, addressing the management of the Second Bank of the United States, which he closed in 1834:

> I have had men watching you for a long time and I am convinced that you have used the funds of the bank to speculate in the breadstuffs of the country. When you won, you divided the profits amongst you, and when you lost, you charged it to the Bank. . . . You are a den of vipers and thieves.

The difference is that today the stakes are bigger in a world of greater connectivity and speed than that in which Old Hickory (as the pugnacious president was aptly nicknamed) operated. Harvard scholar Dani Rodrik has dubbed the rich, connected, and canny überclass the "mobile minority," while the rest who are stuck holding the bag (and also immobile in literal, geographic terms) are the "immobile majority."

Other forms of public-level support for private, profit-making individuals and institutions can be less obvious but no less costly. One thinks of protections or outright payments given to farmers in the United States and Europe (in contrast to Canada and Australia), to zombie banks and companies in Japan, or to automotive manufacturers in many markets. This is no way to run a successful economy, and we're doing more and more of it.

Indian-born Columbia University economist Jagdish Bhagwati describes our market economy as having diverged from Schumpeter's idea of healthy "creative destruction" that sweeps away dying companies and industries to make way for new ones to a distinctly unhealthy "destructive creation," where massive amounts of brainpower and creativity are deployed to game the system. Capital is more instantaneously mobile than ever, while the wreckage of failures is left for everyone else to clean up. Just ask a German taxpayer how he or she likes underwriting the losses and inefficiencies of the Greek and Spanish economies, or whether a Silicon Valley entrepreneur can afford to stay the course in California, with its serial crises, litigation culture, and legendary red tape.

Successive bailouts and stimulus packages, combined with economic weakness and demographic pressures, are pushing the situation to a new tipping point. To be sure, public balance sheets look bad today, with debt levels in the developed world pushing their postwar records (as a percentage of economic activity). But the situation today is positively rosy when compared with the unfunded mandates of retirement support and healthcare for older-growing populations that will be supported by shrinking working-age cohorts. Standard & Poor's, when downgrading the credit ratings of the United States and several European countries, noted as much: It was less about the debt levels today and more about the fact that political courage and intelligent, workable solutions were noticeably absent from the public debate about how to deal with problems that are just around the corner. Projected slow growth doesn't help either, and the relentless barrage of newly released, often seemingly contradictory economic data leaves traders frantic, business leaders uncertain, and politicians bewildered.

The once universally admired Alan Greenspan tried to be helpful during the last U.S. debt-ceiling crisis by stating, "The United States can pay any debt it has because we can always print money to do that. So there is zero probability of default." What such printed money will eventually be worth and who will want to hold it is another question.

The once universally admired Alan Greenspan tried to be helpful during the last U.S. debt-ceiling crisis by stating, "The United States can pay any debt it has because we can always print money to do that. So there is zero probability of default." What such printed money will eventually be worth and who will want to hold it is another question. Anglo-Canadian financier Sir Christopher Ondaatje (whose brother is Michael Ondaatje, author of *The English Patient*) takes a different point of view from Greenspan, saying "The Chinese invention of fiat money [in the tenth century]—paper that is negotiable for goods just because the government says so—was a fruitful but potentially dangerous innovation . . . [leading to] the abuse of paper." Born in colonial Ceylon (now Sri Lanka), Sir Christopher and his brother know a thing or two about what it means to have to start life over again from scratch, as the full faith and credit of any particular government or company may not turn out to be worth the paper it's written on.

In the face of public services cuts and growing income inequality, citizens are increasingly less likely to bear the burdens that our present system requires of them. Faced with a choice between the general benefits of free trade and the market economy, but at the price of sacrificing personal social security plans or healthcare benefits, or the tangible payback of soaking the rich and protecting jobs from foreign competition, who knows what the decision could be. Will we find ways to promote growth while protecting social welfare promises? Will we double down on what passes for laissez-faire capitalism and hope that it doesn't blow up in our faces? No less than the future of the open economy could be at stake, and the choices that we make now will determine the path we ultimately take.

Now it does seem reasonable to ask those who have benefited most over the past several decades to shoulder their fair share of the burden during this period of continuing choppy times. In the UK, the Conservative-led coalition government initially decided to keep the top income tax rate at 50 percent, not counting all the country's other taxes—on capital gains, inheritance, VAT of 20 percent on goods and services bought, excise taxes, local Council (i.e., community) taxes, stamp duty on securities and property transactions, and, yes, 42.5 percent tax on dividends for higher earners. But more than a trickle of the country's entrepreneurs and executives have been voting with their feet, and are leaving the country—to tax-friendly Ireland and Switzerland, among other jurisdictions. One of the favored landing spots of the rich and mobile London financial set is Switzerland's Municipality of Freienbach on Lake Zurich. Though close to the amenities of the city and Zurich's immaculate Kloten airport, it's actually located in neighboring Canton Schwyz, where top marginal tax rates are 11.8 percent (corporate), 19 percent (personal), and 10 percent (on dividends).

I admit it's a conundrum: Raise taxes on the most fortunate in fairness to the rest, and the former will take their talent and capital somewhere else. Newly-elected French President François Hollande has proposed raising the top tax rate in France to 75 percent, which I expect most people elsewhere would regard as an extreme position. (By comparison, the U.S. debate on the Buffett Tax, by which America's rich would be obliged to pay tax at rates no lower than those paid by the middle class, is rather modest.) Pre-Margaret Thatcher Britain in the 1970s had even higher tax rates, and it wasn't only pinstriped bankers who were heading for the exit doors. In a 2002 *Fortune* interview, Rolling Stones guitarist Keith Richards described the band's exodus from Britain and their constant eye on tax issues. With a lit Marlboro and vodka and juice in hand, Richards said, "It's why we rehearse a lot in Canada and not in the United States. A lot of our astute moves have been basically keeping up with tax laws, where to go, and where not to put it. . . . We left England because we'd be paying 98 cents on the dollar. We left, and they lost out . . . and Mick [who attended the London School of Economics] likes to run a pretty tight ship."

It's a dilemma of our time that policy makers must be seen as either pro-business or pro-worker, as though one group could exist without the other. The challenge is that governments—and by extension their citizens—need to think bigger. The choice need not be between attracting business with beggar-thy-neighbor tax policies or punitive tax rates that drive away all but favored national champions who cut special deals. Taxes are important to businesses, but so is a range of other factors as well. Apple employees based in California would realize a clear tax advantage if the company were to relocate them from Cupertino to the suburbs of Las Vegas, but the pool of creative, technologically sophisticated human capital that is so vital to their business has a critical mass in Northern California. (Apple itself has admittedly already taken every possible step to minimize U.S. and California taxes using Dutch, Irish, Nevadan, and other legal structures.)

Poll a group of executives in the United States or UK and find out which is of greater concern for them: failing educational systems, decrepit infrastructure, government insolvency, burdensome regulations, or a modest increase in the marginal tax rate. In fact, the Bay Area

Council Economic Institute (in conjunction with A.T. Kearney) conducted a study in 2004 to look into the reasons why companies with high brainpower needs locate (or stay put) in the high-tax, high-regulation environment of Silicon Valley. The answer? The physical concentration of entrepreneurial culture, advanced technology, and cross-disciplinary research hubs all trumped high taxes and clogged roads.

The Three Deficits

Times like this call out for inspired (and inspiring) leadership, but we haven't been so lucky. Paul Volcker was right: Of the three deficits, the budget deficit and the trade deficit are relatively easier to handle than the arguably more acute leadership deficit. As Volcker wrote in 2005, long before financial crises were on most people's radar: "Altogether the circumstances seem to me as dangerous and intractable as any I can remember, and I can remember quite a lot. What really concerns me is that there seems to be so little willingness or capacity to do much about it."

Unfortunately the steps required for someone to get promoted or elected to a top leadership role in government, business, or civil society today have little to do with the qualities actually needed to be an effective leader, including personal courage and the ability to articulate a vision of the future that inspires and unites for effective and purposeful action.

The importance of this point cannot be underestimated during a period in which most observers feel that bold political action could solve—or at least mitigate—many of the developed world's most pressing challenges, with the alternative—indecision and inaction—able to make them immeasurably worse. One is reminded of the quote by Luxembourg Prime Minister and sometime European Council President Jean-Claude Junker, highlighted at the beginning of this chapter, about how we know what we need to do, but we don't know how to get re-elected once we've done it. One struggles to see Franklin Roosevelt, John F. Kennedy, Winston Churchill, or Charles de Gaulle taking such a position. Each of those leaders at times was driven to espouse policies that were sharply unpopular in the short term, but they were confident that over time their positions would come to be appreciated by voters.

Today's political process frustrates this type of bold and farsighted political action and the selection of leaders who are likely to take it. In a 24-hour news cycle world, even the most skilled and media-savvy leaders find it very difficult to keep their control over messaging. The time and public deliberation necessary to explain and debate complex policy positions and solutions is cut short, replaced by the need to produce 30-second sound bites. Is it any wonder that the tough questions of entitlement reform and competitiveness are almost exclusively discussed by academics, while elected leaders focus instead on simpler, highly emotive—yet ultimately less consequential—issues? And it doesn't help that the issues confronting a globalized, multipolar world are inherently more complex than those in the past.

Because the ability to produce short, catchy, telegenic sound bites that resonate emotionally with voters has become a critical success factor in modern politics, we inevitably select leaders who meet this criterion—regardless of whether they fall short in many (or sometimes all) other areas. Statesmanship and the command of complex policy issues are qualities in a candidate that are regularly dismissed as sure signs of being out-of-touch. Additionally, practicing the essential art of statecraft in the form of the compromise only opens candidates from any place on the political spectrum to attack from partisans at the more extreme fringes.

On the rare occasion that a capable mind successfully navigates the labyrinth of the electoral process, they are then rewarded by facing the Minotaur of character assassination. In my view, Bill Clinton was one of the most thoughtful and intelligent political thinkers of the past 50 years, but he was forced to spend too much of his presidency responding to attacks on his (admittedly too colorful) personal life. The amount of time devoted to the facts and circumstances surrounding President Barack Obama's birth illustrates the same trend, as did the tabloid fascination with French President Nicolas Sarkozy's marriage. If the press had spent its time digging into what we now know to be

JFK's extra-curricular activities, would the distraction have meant that the highly dangerous Cuban missile crisis or the move toward enhanced civil rights might have ended differently?

I admit that I have some strong views on all this. I was there, in the U.S. Congress, that momentous day in 1979 when the proceedings of the House of Representatives became televised for the first time, and TV make-up kits were literally passed out like candy. Less than a decade later, the Senate followed, helping transform what was arguably the world's greatest deliberative body into a hotbed of posturing. Members of Congress who used to go to the cloakroom principally to consult and seek important compromise on critical public policy issues now all too often go through those doors to powder their noses for the klieg lights.

In the late 1970s and early 1980s, I worked as legislative director for then Senator Joe Biden of Delaware, now, of course, U.S. Vice President. Few remember him today as the young, extraordinarily bright, newly elected senator who had—against all odds—defeated the well-loved, incumbent, senior Republican Senator from Delaware, Caleb Boggs. Joe's life had been marred by great tragedy just weeks after his election: His wife and youngest child were killed in a car accident—hit by a tractor-trailer—and his two sons were seriously injured. He considered resigning to care for them, but was persuaded to stay by then Senate Majority Leader Mike Mansfield (D-Montana), as Joe commuted between Washington and Delaware every day to be home at night with his boys. The boys eventually made full recoveries and are now quite impressive and successful in their public- and private-sector activities.

Though sometimes ribbed for being verbose, Joe was, and is, in fact, among the best at making a case clearly, succinctly, and compellingly. At the time of this writing, he has made the case for the Obama presidency with bumper sticker simplicity: "Osama bin Laden is dead, and General Motors is alive." Not a bad line. In considering contentious issues, he used to quickly distill the most complex and thorny subjects by asking two top experts with opposing views to join him and to debate one another—and it's still a good way of probing difficult problems. And those who come to know Joe Biden, as I was fortunate enough to do early in my career, find his deep values, uncanny intelligence, and commitment to delivering on the needs of people inspiring and irresistible.

During those years, I also got to know many other senators. I observed newly elected Senator Bill Bradley of New Jersey work diligently to learn the parliamentary procedure of the Senate after he arrived. Ever the meticulous Rhodes Scholar and former professional basketball player, he studied the Senate rules in much the same way he reportedly mapped out the perfect shot to the hoop as a former star New York Knick. How many new legislators today take the time to immerse themselves in the rules and customs of the body in which they've been elected to serve? Not many, I think. Quite a few go straight to grandstanding within hours of their arrival.

It also hasn't helped that problems and opportunities are increasingly long-term and cross-border, while political cycles get shorter and more sharply parochial. This is a fairly fundamental problem: The technological complexity and speed that has driven global interdependency, making nearly every political issue more difficult but also more impactful, has created a system in which politicians and voters are encouraged to think more locally and shorter-term. Promoting economic competitiveness, for example, has always required a fundamental vision of a country's position, interests, and strategy over the long term in the context of the wider world. But voters and politicians seem interested primarily in achieving immediate—if illusory—gains for specific interest groups in the local electorate. This asymmetry of time and space holds long-term national and, indeed, global concerns hostage to petty squabbles that only look to the next election, if even that far.

The trouble is that our long-term national and global problems are real, and the political systems that are in place simply can't keep up. This contributes to the deplorable rise in partisanship seen in so many countries. The short-term, local way of dealing with complex, long-term, bigger issues is not working, and because leaders lack solutions and the ability to find solutions, they revert to the survival mechanism of attacking one another. Voters, who should be the ultimate arbiters of political discourse in democratic societies, are instead tuning out, frustrated by the massive financial and organizational hurdles required to navigate the political process and disgusted with the choices that process yields. This seeming political myopia, however, should not be a total surprise, nor can we fully blame our political officials for short-termism. The simple fact is that in an increasingly borderless—or flat world—the benefits of integration are often diffuse and long-term, whereas the pain of dislocation in globalization's wake is immediate and palpable. This creates, at best, complicated politics, requiring extraordinarily deft leadership and equally open and generous followership—both in short supply these days. It's what the behavioral economists also call loss aversion—given a choice individuals are often more likely to opt to hold on to what they have, rather than risk it for something better.

Of course in most countries, a career in public service offers that unbeatable package of low pay, long hours, great intrusion into one's private life, and restrictions on what you can do and earn afterward. What's not to like? Are you surprised if you're not getting the caliber of leader or government official that you want?

The results are striking, as basic leadership—and resultant followership—have been absent in a number of recent crises of different natures and scopes. From the financial crisis, where actions were (and continue to be) indecisive and uncoordinated, to the uprising of the 2011 Arab spring to the Fukushima-Daiichi disaster, crises are less often defined by the bold actions of capable leaders and more often by the confusion and cacophony that they generate. If you're not convinced, try reading the new U.S. law, the Dodd-Frank Act—all 2,600 pages of it, which aims to regulate Wall Street reform in the wake of recent market excesses and financial collapse.

My friend Ambassador Kishore Mahbubani, dean of the Lee Kwan Yew School of Public Policy at the National University of Singapore, calls our situation a rudderless world. (In etiquette-bound Asia, Kishore is just about the most brilliant and plainspoken statesman you can find; he grew up in Singapore's traditionally disadvantaged Indian minority during the last years of British colonial rule, and this vantage point has, I think, given him a unique perspective in this mostly Chinese city-state.) Kishore, of course, would likely be among the first to point out that the gradual loss of Western hegemony is both a product and a cause of increased complexity in global affairs.

As Kishore puts it in his own words:

> In the past, when the billions of citizens of planet earth lived in separated countries, it was like having an ocean of separate boats. Hence, the postwar order created rules to ensure that the boats did not collide; it created rules for cooperation. Up until now, this arrangement has worked well. World War III did not follow World Wars I and II. But today the world's seven billion citizens no longer live in separate boats. They live in more than 190 cabins on the same boat. Each cabin has a government to manage its affairs. And the boat as a whole moves along without a captain or a crew. The world is adrift.

It's not that the nineteenth century Great Game in Central Asia or the Cold War closer to our time were simple—far from it. It's just that by adding the competing interests of a whole new—and massive—field of players from the developing world, that complexity has been magnified exponentially.

Anyway, you know the further story. There are five things that can't be combined without dangerous delusions: aging populations, low taxes, unfunded pensions, rising government spending, and external borrowing. To say the numbers don't add up is a gross understatement. But the clash of raised voices in the developed world's legislative bodies doesn't equal action of any productive kind. In the words of former Chairman of the U.S. Council of Economic Advisors Herbert Stein, "Things that can't go on forever won't."

Leaders in the past have understood this and changed their views when events caught up to them (think of the famous quote of Lord Keynes: "When the facts change, I change my mind. What do you do, sir?"). In France, François Mitterrand was swept into office in 1981 on the platform of "110 Propositions for France"—nationalizations, expansionary fiscal policy, higher taxes on wealth, and the like. He even included Communists in his cabinet. Two years and two franc devaluations later, President Mitterrand abruptly reversed course. His original agenda was wrecking the economy, and he got the message. Bowing to German demands for sharp fiscal consolidation as the price for a desperately needed third franc devaluation, Mitterrand embarked on the *tournant de la rigeur*, which focused on rebuilding competitiveness and fiscal restraint. One struggles to imagine the reaction one of today's leaders would receive from the 24-hour news cycle for a similar show of broad-mindedness. (Critics of Mitterrand did like to point out a lifetime of personal re-invention, from the far right to the hard left and then back to the center during the course of his presidency.)

The trick to governing is always finding good policy that is also good politics. Absent that rare combination, leaders have to weigh the virtues of the two and determine which to place emphasis on, policy or politics. Fiscal austerity in Mitterrand's case was good policy— France was not only able to regain economic momentum, but was also one of the only OECD countries that did not see rising economic inequality during the 1980s. But, at least in the short term, it was not good politics. Mitterrand's leftist coalition lost elections in 1983 and 1984, and in 1986 he was forced into cohabitation, an arrangement in which he had no choice but to share power with a right-of-center prime minister. He did survive, however, and led France until 1995, for an almost unprecedented 14 years.

In today's political world, it's difficult to conceive of a politician choosing good policy that's bad politics. One can envision cable and satellite news relentlessly streaming analysis of a president's or prime minister's flip–flopping, clever catch phrases being flung about on Twitter, viral YouTube videos decrying the decision, and call-in talk shows stirring the pot. Rather than surviving an election cycle with an opportunity to reshape their message, a leader can go from popular to pariah in no time flat. Witness the precipitous decline in the fortunes of British Prime Minister Tony Blair, who made what he genuinely felt was a courageous decision to commit Britain to the Iraq War in the face of public disapproval (it is, of course, debatable whether this was in retrospect good policy, but there's no doubt Blair believed it to be so). Rather than seeking a fourth mandate and cementing the position of New Labour and the Third Way, Blair was forced to resign

The day of reckoning has arrived even faster in some places, threatening key economic nodes like California. Some admirers of the Coast of Dreams believe that it will ultimately transcend every crisis, and even former Mitterrand adviser Jacques Attali takes the view that in California, "The permanent threat of earthquakes gives rise to an intense, unique vibrancy, a fabulous desire to live, and a passion for the new."

early, and his Labour successor (Gordon Brown) was soon driven from Number 10 at the ballot box.

The day of reckoning has arrived even faster in some places, threatening key economic nodes like California. Some admirers of the Coast of Dreams believe that it will ultimately transcend every crisis, and even former Mitterrand adviser Jacques Attali takes the view that in California, "The permanent threat of earthquakes gives rise to an intense, unique vibrancy, a fabulous desire to live, and a passion for the new." Maybe San Francisco and LA just look better from Paris? But California state historian Kevin Starr more accurately describes the once-Golden State as now in a "collective nervous breakdown," with its ungovernable mess of thousands of overlapping counties, cities, and districts. True, it's easier to rethink the social contract between the citizen and state in smaller jurisdictions like Singapore or the Gulf emirates (the contemporary versions of such earlier powerhouses as Venice, Genoa, and the canny Hanseatic trading cities). This may, in fact, be a time of renaissance for the autonomous city-state or special administrative region, as we'll see later in the book. The irony here is that Californians are some of the most democratically over-represented people in the world, given that so many state issues require direct ballot initiatives.

One can see the origins of this leadership vacuum in the 1990s when politicians, including President Bill Clinton and Speaker Newt Gingrich in the United States, were accused of governing by focus group. This charge may not be entirely fair to either man, but it is undeniable that the trend of increasingly sophisticated electoral analytics has contributed to sharp political polarization that has left governments hamstrung across the world. Again, each day, we have an avalanche of new political information and polling data but with no corresponding increase in our capacity to make sense of it and to use it wisely. The wisdom of crowds is, in fact, often nothing of the sort. Walter Winchell's notion that leaders lead by understanding where the public mind is and then helping direct it to where it needs to go is too often today hostage to the dilemma of choosing good policy or good politics. Both Clinton and Gingrich were—and are—what in Washington are referred to, respectfully and with deference, as policy wonks. They both have an encyclopedic command of regulation, economic studies, budgetary reports, and political precedent. No one would be likely to accuse either man of pursuing initiatives that they did not believe were grounded in good policy.

At the same time, both departed from the time-honored tradition of persuading people—other politicians, the electorate—of the (to borrow a phrase central to us at A.T. Kearney) "essential rightness" of their positions through an exposition of the underlying arguments in support of their views. It was only very late in Clinton's first term that the two sides, convinced that the political gridlock which had arisen would be more disastrous politically than either side conceding points to the other, came together to pass the Personal Responsibility and Work Opportunity Act, a signature reform of the U.S. welfare system. You can call it political alchemy if you like, but the shame is that two talented politicians were unable to accomplish more during their times in office, and the effectiveness of both arguably was weakened by their own compromise on values.

The coalition and the art of the compromise has been a building block of the democratic process since the establishment of the office of the Prime Minister of England (referred to then, and still technically now, as the First Lord of the Treasury) ensured the Hanoverian succession in 1688, or since the 1787 Grand Bargain between Northern and Southern U.S. states that resulted in a bicameral House and Senate. Coalition building has always been a process of skillfully weaving together a patchwork of self-interest and differing views and principles under the guise of ideological flexibility. This process has broken down as ideological differences (or at least their appearance) have sharpened, and self-interest is defined more by sound-bite victories and less by policy-level successes. One need only look to the U.S. fiscal outlook or the (cloudy) future of the Eurozone to see the effects of coalition-free, compromise-deprived democracy.

Beyond what I have outlined, some analysts including Moisés Naím see one additional kicker to the loud, fractious, and unproductive politics of today. As Moisés says: "To put it simply: Power no longer buys as much as it did in the past. In the 21st century, power is easier to get, harder to use . . . and easier to lose. From boardrooms and combat zones to cyberspace, battles for power are as intense as ever, but they are yielding diminishing returns. Their fierceness masks the ever more evanescent nature of power itself. And understanding how power dissipates and is losing its value is the hidden key to making sense of the most important trends reshaping the world in the early 21st century, and facing up to the hard challenges they pose."

Inescapable Trilemma?

Last year I traveled to Shanghai with a group of client CEOs and assorted luminaries, including renowned political scientist Francis Fukuyama. Frank made a very interesting point: We don't know how to turn Afghanistan into Denmark, nor do we know how to unparalyze representative democracy around the world. (He also made the point that few of us know how "Denmark turned into Denmark," that is, how—over a thousand years—assorted tribes of Nordic marauders and Viking thugs managed to become a peaceable and prosperous democratic country; if you want to understand just how it happened, read Frank's latest book.)

Turkish-born Harvard professor Dani Rodrik, whom I cited earlier, regularly makes a point that is equally thought provoking: Is it possible to have, simultaneously, democratic mass politics, national sovereignty, and an open global economy? He thinks the answer is clearly no, and calls it the inescapable trilemma: You can have two of the three, but not all three. Try to have all three at once, and what you get is the messy gridlock that lurches from election campaign shouting matches to overhyped boom to economic crisis and back again. If he's right (a scary thought), remedies for fixing Washington (or saving the European Union) are missing the point. Silicon Valley billionaire Peter Thiel, the libertarian cofounder of PayPal and early investor in Facebook and LinkedIn, puts Rodrik's trilemma in slightly different (and even more ominous) terms, saying, "I no longer believe that freedom and democracy are compatible."

The Case for Values-Based Leadership

Unlike Peter Thiel, I continue to believe that freedom and democracy are compatible, but that freedom, democracy, and capitalism can only function when all of the actors in the system accept a clear sense of responsibility—to themselves, to one another, and to the planet. Responsibility, to be effective, cannot be handed down and enforced—it must come from a system of values.

Values is an over-used (and perhaps "loaded") word these days, but I don't shy away from it when and where it's needed. Simply put, we need to move from a world and a system in which people do good by doing well—that is, benefit others and the planet only as a byproduct of focusing on personal profit—to a system in which one does well by doing good—when providing true leadership and service is the central priority and financial returns and personal enrichment are merely their corollaries.

Doing good is no longer an end of doing well—much as it might have been in the 1970s when I began my professional career in the oil industry. Then, one was compelled to do good in order to nurture favor with constituencies critical to the achievement of core corporate objectives. Today's world, transformed by ubiquitous technologies bridging time and space, ensures that corporate behavior no longer just impacts shareholders, but in very important ways also touches the legitimate needs, desires, and welfare of broad groups of stakeholders—consumers, communities, and voters extending far beyond the traditional 10K statement.

Today's world, transformed by ubiquitous technologies bridging time and space, ensures that corporate behavior no longer just impacts shareholders, but in very important ways also touches the legitimate needs, desires, and welfare of broad groups of stakeholders—consumers, communities, and voters extending far beyond the traditional 10K statement.

I know that this is anathema for many economists. I studied at the University of Chicago, the home of the late Milton Friedman, who was one of the more passionate advocates of the notion that businesses have a sole responsibility to focus on financial returns, because their one and only societal role is to create wealth. It's not that Friedman embraced a Gordon Gekko-style, greed-is-good ethos, but that he genuinely believed in the underlying economic principles. As Friedman wrote in his influential 1962 book *Capitalism and Freedom*: "There is one and only one social responsibility of business: to use its resources to engage in activities designed to increase its profits so long as it stays within the rules of the game, which is to say, engages in open and free competition, without deception or fraud."

Although Friedman made important contributions to the field of economics, the bottom line is that this theory on the sole purpose of business enterprise has not turned out to be correct—or indeed healthy. It has not worked for society, which continues to be beset by corruption, scandals, and breaches of trust, and it has not worked for a number of companies and their shareholders. In fact, the intellectual father of capitalism, eighteenth-century Scottish thinker Adam Smith, is too well remembered today for such phrases as "the invisible hand." In truth, Smith's legacy has been grossly oversimplified: He was a dogged advocate of the view that free enterprise absolutely required strong moral and ethical underpinnings and that most market participants needed to be people of (to use his words) propriety, prudence, and benevolence in order for the system to work properly. Smith, of course, is best known for his book *The Wealth of Nations*, which many consider to be the founding document of free-market capitalism. But Smith himself is thought to have placed greater value on his earlier work, *The Theory of Moral Sentiments*, in which he explores the ability to think and act morally in the face of pure natural self-interest. Despite completing *The Theory of Moral Sentiments* 17 years before *The Wealth of Nations*, Smith continued to revise the former until his death in 1790. In fact, despite the fact that the bulk of his contemporary and posthumous fame was derived from *The Wealth of Nations*, his gravestone lists his authorship of that work second.

John Kay, who was founding head of Oxford's new business school in 1996, calls this paradox *obliquity*: Just as you can't find happiness by looking for

> *[Adam] Smith's legacy has been grossly over-simplified: He was a dogged advocate of the view that free enterprise absolutely required strong moral and ethical underpinnings and that most market participants needed to be people of (to use his words) propriety, prudence, and benevolence in order for the system to work properly.*

it desperately, you can't be profitable by relentlessly pursuing profits. Profits—as well as happiness—come to those who pursue other things first; for example, creating amazing products, elevating client or customer service to a new high, helping a colleague, blazing a new trail, or teaching a child to read.

Doing well by doing good and a commitment to leading by placing values first are cultural pillars of my firm, A.T. Kearney. We were the first major consulting firm to commit to embed sustainability in all that we do for our clients and ourselves, and the first so-called high-value-added management consulting firm to reach a stated goal of carbon neutrality. We committed to both of these initiatives without commercial pretensions—at the time sustainability was seen by many as a fad, and carbon neutrality too often conjured up little more than images of buying expensive offset credits for PR purposes. Yet we undertook both because we felt as a firm that they were the *right*—and *smart*—things to do, for our clients and for society—and six years later, we have been rewarded for both. A commitment to sustainability perfectly represents the intersection of doing well by doing good. Sustainability is the doing well by doing good sweet spot. It is the place where the pursuit of profit blends seamlessly with the pursuit of the common good. A commitment to sustainability is all about fulfilling a company's ambitions to be profitable while delivering on society's need to conserve resources and protect the environment at the same time.

Maintaining a commitment to values is not always easy, and the choices are not always straightforward. Google, whose informal corporate motto is "Don't Be Evil," found this out a few years back when it encountered censorship issues with its business in China. Google faced a choice between offering users in China access to its U.S.-based Google.com site or establishing a local Google.cn branch. The former offered Chinese users access to the full Google-sphere, but because it had to pass through China's so-called great firewall, the user experience was rather slow and the government censored a number of search terms. Opening a Google.cn site would improve speed and reliability, but Google had to agree to self-censor content. Google's mission statement stresses that "Google's mission is to organize the world's information and make it universally accessible and useful." Clearly censorship was an activity in violation of the group's founding principles. When shareholders protested, Google was faced with a choice between violating its principles and exiting the world's largest (by population) market. One can debate the merit of Google's eventual solution—to maintain a self-censored Google.cn while offering a link to an uncensored Google.com.hk based in Hong Kong—but the complexities that can arise when principles and the real world meet are clearly there.

Early in my tenure as chairman and CEO of A.T. Kearney, we faced a critical test when we concluded that two of our highest-performing partners were acting in ways that we believed were inconsistent with our firm's principles, culture, and values. We were presented with what some thought a difficult choice. In the midst of the financial crisis and our own fragile post-MBO financial position, there was significant pressure to meet our profitability needs, and removing high performers was bound to have a negative impact, at least initially, on shareholder interests. However, we felt more strongly that it was an imperative to stay true to our principles and maintain a trust- and values-based partnership, and our trust in these partners had been compromised. So, during the height of the greatest economic turmoil in any of our lifetimes, those partners, who were two of our best commercial performers, left our firm. Four years on, our firm has prospered, able to continue to serve our clients effectively with a partner group even more fully aligned and passionately committed to the core principles and values on which our firm was built. I can't think of a clearer example of addition through subtraction. This unalterable commitment to our values in all that we do undoubtedly explains why in the process of this journey we have enjoyed the highest employee engagement scores in our profession.

Chapter 4

Lighten the Load and Make It *Sesame Street* Simple

Watch out for a new brand of consumer . . . surrounded by too much stuff . . . increasingly skeptical in the face of a financial meltdown that it was all worth the effort. Out will go luxury purchases, conspicuous consumption, and a trophy culture. Tomorrow's consumer will buy more ephemeral, less cluttering stuff: fleeting, but expensive, experiences, not heavy goods for the home.

—John Quelch, Dean, China Europe International Business School (CEIBS), Shanghai and Non-Executive Director, WPP PLC

I have very few possessions . . . a few papers, a couple of books, and a few shirts, jackets, sweaters. It fits in a little thing, in a paper bag, so it's very easy.

—Nicolas Berggruen, billionaire investor and Chairman of Berggruen Holdings

There are a number of ways we are lightening the load and dematerializing goods and information, as this evolution shows. Printed books were literally state-of-the-art for more than 600 years, while the CD-ROM and flash drive have been blink-of-an-eye stepping stones to the even lighter—and invisible—cloud storage.
SOURCE: Bix Burkhart/Photographer's Choice/Getty Images.

In the developed world, we are choking on stuff as well as on information: In recent years, self-storage has been one of the fastest-growing businesses, as people in even super-sized homes run out of space for their accumulating junk. It's not a pretty stereotype, but the 1990s image of a Hummer driver stuck in traffic and slurping down empty calories had some truth to it. Despite how it may have seemed at the time, this was not progress, but actually a really unhealthy way to live for both people and the planet.

But don't just take my word for it. The group Global Footprint Network has developed a way of measuring the ecological demands of global consumption and output in terms of how many planet Earths these activities consume. Right now, we're using the resources of about one-and-a-half planets to maintain current consumption levels. These researchers predict that under current trends (which of course can— and, one may say, must—change) we will need more than two planets by 2050. And the consumption levels are very uneven across countries: Americans have an average ecological footprint of 23 acres, whereas Europeans require about half as much, and Bengalis just 1.25 acres. And what has greater resource consumption done for citizens of the developed world? While we obviously enjoy higher income levels, we also experience other sorts of growth, with the Organisation for Economic Co-operation and Development (OECD) estimating obesity rates in the United States at 33.8 percent, the United Kingdom at 23 percent, and the comparatively slim Spanish and Germans at about 13 percent.

Perhaps the recent downturn, for all its many ills, will drive a reassessment of priorities. During the depths of the global financial crisis in late 2008, writers Venetia Thompson and Rory Sutherland listed "the pointless luxuries and trends that will, quite rightly, be culled by the recession," arguing that "capitalism is at its indisputable best not when picking but when picking off. . . . In unerringly killing off the bad: the inefficient, the redundant, the outdated or the needlessly complex." They went on to write in Britain's *Spectator* magazine, "Along with great increases in wealth and industry, the last 15 years of growth have seen a steady accumulation of pointless and unproductive forms of human activity: witless expenditure, insane trends and bizarre herd behaviors."

According to Thompson and Sutherland, such boom-era activities on the way out include "property porn" ("the unquestioned assumption . . . that home improvement is the highest form of self improvement"), the one-upmanship of vacations "to increasingly far-flung and dangerous parts of the world," "insane working hours," "the veneration of financial services," and the mania for buying second (and third and fourth) homes ("Do you want to spend your precious fortnight's holiday practicing the [local language] for 'My septic tank appears to have exploded?'"). A bit harsh? Yes. But there is some truth to their biting commentary.

During times of robust growth, I'll admit that most of us get a bit carried away. In the so-called go-go years and bull markets of the post-World War II era, many thought the biggest challenge of the future was going to be how to fill our vast amounts of leisure time. (Did they ever get that one wrong.)

During times of robust growth, I'll admit that most of us get a bit carried away. In the so-called go-go years and bull markets of the post-World War II era, many thought the biggest challenge of the future was going to be how to fill our vast amounts of leisure time. (Did they ever get that one wrong.) During our last boom, I came across promotional literature for a real estate development in Hawaii called Ka'anapali Coffee Farms: "Picture life in a magical West Maui setting. Acres of green give way to endless Pacific views. Gentle rains and mauka breezes refresh the sunlit days and quiet nights. Because the farming on your 4-to-7 acre coffee estate is entirely managed by local growers, you'll have time to enjoy your home in paradise. . . ." The prospect of being a boutique coffee planter in Maui is, to be sure, a unique twist on property development. In the early 2000s, it all seemed very possible, even affordable (if you extrapolated real estate values and economic growth). I will give the Ka'anapali folks credit for their staying power, as many such real estate developments have gone bust since 2007.

So we've come back down to earth. In both the developed and developing world, there is a shift in consumer values toward what I call "Simplicity, Sustainability, and Self-fulfillment." Simplicity we have covered already—a drive toward the comprehensible and manageable in a world of bewildering complexity (again, this should not be confused with low-tech, as the success of Apple's cutting-edge but easy-to-use products demonstrate). Sustainability is a trend that most analysts thought would evaporate with the economic downturn, but that forecast has failed to materialize in the face of growing awareness about the social and environmental impacts of consumption. Self-fulfillment reflects a shift from material to experience-based consumption, both for enjoyment and health reasons.

As evidence, look no further than the burgeoning popularity of yoga. Once considered a fringe (and rather expensive) activity, yoga's popularity in the United States grew by 20 percent per year during the financial crisis and reached annual sales of $6.5 billion in 2011. While it's easy to call out examples of each of these three themes in various marketing campaigns, it's important to recognize that these three trends are in fact mutually reinforcing. Pursuing simplicity, for example, in product design, production, materials, packaging, and lifestyle leads to sustainability and a less cluttered, potentially more fulfilling lifestyle.

Apple has successfully hit on all of these themes with products that are striking in their elegant simplicity—both in terms of appearance and in their use, more recyclable and eco-friendly than other competing products, and made to be easy and enjoyable to use. Journalist and scientist Matt Ridley makes a special point about the wonderful deflation in Apple products, saying in the *Wall Street Journal,* "An iPhone, for example, weighs 1/100th and costs 1/10th as much as an Osborne Executive computer did in 1982, but it has 150 times the processing speed and 100,000 times the memory."

The bike-sharing movement that has sprung up in a number of major cities in the United States and Europe follows a similar pattern. These programs deliver simplicity by being easy to use (your membership in the program entitles you to simply ride any available bike and drop it off at any stand), and by simplifying lifestyles that no longer depend on vehicle fees, parking, and so on. They are sustainable by swapping out carbon-emitting vehicles for zero-emission bicycles. Finally, they contribute to the lifestyle by promoting physical fitness and reducing traffic jams and extra expense. London's flamboyant, tow-headed mayor Boris Johnson has been seen biking (in a business suit) around the British capital to promote the Barclays Cycle Hire program, and I admit it's a brave cyclist who is willing to ride in London's heavy traffic. But look carefully and I think that you will find that more and more of the most successful advertising campaigns and products are following this framework.

We are dematerializing our manufactures as aircraft, cars, homes, and white goods get lighter, use less material, and sip (rather than guzzle) fuel and electricity. And many people prefer to buy not more physical stuff, but rather life experiences: travel, education, entertainment, wellness, and so on. As the saying goes, you can't take it with you.

This transformation represents welcome news: Consumers and companies have gotten the message that we need to lighten our load, and we're doing so thanks to a new generation of technological innovations. We are dematerializing our manufactures as aircraft, cars, homes, and white goods get lighter, use less material, and sip (rather than guzzle) fuel and electricity. And many people prefer to buy not more physical stuff, but rather life experiences: travel, education, entertainment, wellness, and so on. As the saying goes, you can't take it with you. And new consumers aren't even sure they actually need or want to own what they operate—as the Zipcar experience suggests. Unsurprisingly, U.S. gasoline consumption has dropped from a post-war high of over 460 gallons per capita a year to recent levels in the 430 gallon range. It's a far cry from what many would consider consistent with sustainability, but it's an improvement nonetheless.

The car-sharing idea was, by the way, developed in Switzerland, where car prices, fuel costs, and parking charges are sky-high. But the origins of this concept have more humble beginnings in the vacation timesharing market; even now, the term timeshare has something of a negative, down-market stigma about it. By the time the idea hit the classier private jet market, it was dubbed fractional ownership. And, if priced correctly, such arrangements (including leasing and pay per view) can be more economically efficient than outright ownership.

Sesame Street Simple

As an antidote to what I've described, lots of businesses and consumers have generated a groundswell of enthusiasm for simplicity—in products, in lifestyles, and in operations. Former P&G chairman A. G. Lafley memorably describes this as the move to *Sesame Street* Simple. The successful companies (and political units) of the present and near future are those that delight and simplify choice for the harried and stressed-out consumer—as Apple has done with a truly beautiful-to-behold product line small enough to be laid out on a single table. Behavioral scientist Barry Schwartz at brainy Swarthmore College outside Philadelphia has closely studied what he appropriately calls the "Paradox of Choice": how an excessive abundance of choices and options in every aspect of life—from the mundane to the momentous—causes anxiety, creates perpetual stress, and actually diminishes our sense of well-being. The best companies of our time already get this, and help edit and curate their offerings so the consumer doesn't have be overwhelmed or spend vast amounts of time sorting through every possibility. Those selling products and services that remain stuck in a world of paralyzing options, clunky design, cumbersome movement, discomfort, and pure drudgery will increasingly be toast.

Those selling products and services that remain stuck in a world of paralyzing options, clunky design, cumbersome movement, discomfort, and pure drudgery will increasingly be toast.

Sir Martin Sorrell, the man who built the WPP Group into the world's most potent force in marketing services, makes the case in fewer than 20 words: ". . . We live in an information-rich world. Make something too complicated to understand and we'll turn off the receptors." If, like Sir Martin, you have spent a lifetime buying up the greatest agencies in advertising and PR, from the original "Mad Men" of Ogilvy & Mather, J. Walter Thompson, Grey, and Young & Rubicam to Hill & Knowlton and Burson-Marsteller, the last thing you want anybody to do is turn off their receptors.

Serial entrepreneur (and good friend) Brett Markinson, who recently sold his members-only, private sale website HauteLook to notably well-run retailer Nordstrom for $270 million, takes the view that highly personalized, curated (and truly enjoyable and entertaining) customer experiences are the future—and that we are only at the very beginning of that evolution, since the Internet and its associated technologies are still only in their infancy. (Brett is also part of a growing community of successful business leaders drawn to the unique, creative, and saner—even if zanier to some—lifestyle of the City Different, as Santa Fe calls itself.)

As Brett says,

We are moving from an era of "intent"-based shopping to an era of "discovery and entertainment"-based shopping, a transformation being driven by the evolution in the devices we use. The first wave of Internet shopping took place on the desktop. You might call this a "lean-forward" environment, where tasks and work get done. Now smartphones and "lean-back" tablet devices are making the customer experience much more dynamic, even blending online with a traditional trip to the shopping mall. But regardless of the device, next-generation shopping will be all about intuitive engagement—and enjoyment. In the future, you will be drawn in and helped along by firms that have your permission to anticipate what you might want or what might tickle your fancy—even before the thoughts occur to you. Companies that understand this, and can execute with creativity, simplicity, fun, and true personalization, will be many steps ahead of the rest.

Earlier in the book I cited both Apple and Volkswagen as examples of corporations that get it regarding simplicity and in two very different ways. Whereas Apple has mastered simple design and product function, VW has developed a way to produce vehicles across a number of brands using just four vehicle platforms.

Okay, you say, it's relatively easy for Procter & Gamble, Apple, Nordstrom, or Volkswagen to simplify things and curate creatively, but what can governments do, with an ever-growing and mind-numbing number of laws, regulations, and overlapping jurisdictions? While I wouldn't want to hold up the UK as a shining example in all areas, it has been one of many countries where e-government is making a difference. British citizens have the easy-to-use, one-stop Directgov website, where they can pay taxes, choose a school, apply for a driver's license, register to vote—or even report a crime.

At A.T. Kearney we have worked extensively with public-sector clients to help them embed what we call agile government. Our research has led us to identify six aspects that governments need to target to achieve agility:

- Leadership.
- Organizational change.
- e-Government.
- Customer service.
- Performance management.
- Culture and values.

Before you roll your eyes at these management concepts for governments, please think of what it would actually be like for your

While I wouldn't want to hold up the UK as a shining example in all areas, it has been one of many countries where e-government is making a difference. British citizens have the easy-to-use, one-stop Directgov website, where they can pay taxes, choose a school, apply for a driver's license, register to vote—or even report a crime.

interactions with some government agency (say the IRS in the United States or the similarly named Inland Revenue in Britain, or a motor vehicle bureau virtually anywhere) to be really simple, efficient, fast, and even, well, enjoyable. It's probably not something you've ever experienced before, but if I can do something about it, it's coming soon to a government near you.

One challenge is that as an organization—be it public or private sector—expands in size, it also grows in terms of the number of stakeholders it must satisfy. Governments are particularly susceptible to this challenge, as by definition they are intended to be responsive to a whole cacophony of interests, and simplicity for one person could feel like disenfranchise-ment for another.

The simplicity movement I'm describing is in many ways an instinctive reaction to the complexity and chaos in life generated by the information smog—the question is whether it can succeed on a large enough scale to make a difference beyond the success of individual companies and some intelligent governments. However, for the moment, innovations are bubbling up, and one business school has become a key hub for this kind of thinking: the University of Toronto's Rotman School. A few years ago, Toronto was not on anybody's list of top B-schools, so they had to do something distinctive and high-powered to get noticed. And so they did. Thanks to a visionary dean, Roger Martin, Rotman has become a hub of integrative thinking, bringing together the entire palette of business disciplines with the field of design—industrial, product, information, and visual. If you haven't checked it out, I recommend a visit.

Cockpit Confusion

Now, you may be saying to yourself, information overload and messiness is annoying and sometimes overwhelming, but it's not life-or-death. Actually it can be life-or-death. You may recall the tragic story of Air France Flight 447, which crashed into the Atlantic Ocean in 2009 with a loss of all on board—228 passengers and crew who were traveling from Rio to Paris. Like many people, I was originally mystified by the news: Air France has a very good safety and maintenance record, the plane was a relatively new Airbus A330 (which is a superb piece of equipment), and the nasty equatorial storms of the flight path—with fast-moving 60,000-foot thunderheads—are navigated safely by flights every day. Even the freezing up of the pitot tubes, which measure airspeed, is something pilots are trained to handle.

What we now know, following the recovery of the black boxes from the ocean floor, is that the two first officers on the flight deck were simply overwhelmed by the non-stop cascade of faults, alarms, and warnings in really hairy nighttime flying conditions and the need to fly the plane manually—the autopilot had switched itself off with the loss of airspeed readings. In theory, these circumstances should have been survivable, with the pilots regaining control of the situation and continuing to fly on safely. The arguments over whether the crash was primarily due to pilot error are still going on, but it seems clear that cockpit confusion was a major factor in the disaster. First Officers David Robert and Pierre-Cedric Bonin apparently couldn't, in the mounting chaos of the moment, figure out what was essential to do next.

If that's a problem on a commercial airliner's flight deck, you can imagine it's an even more serious problem on the battlefield. Armies around the world are now trying to develop technologies that help individual soldiers process absolutely essential information in the chaos and heat of battle and screen out everything else that's extraneous. In short, simplify and clarify what the soldier on the ground needs to know, and do it instantaneously. The intention is to help soldiers take in critical battlefield inputs in real time, in order to allow them to act more quickly, decisively, and effectively—and, one hopes, minimize civilian deaths and damage, and mistakes from so-called friendly fire. To quote a U.S. Air Force general, "The B-52 [bomber] lived and died on the quality of its sheet metal. Today our aircraft will live or die on the quality of our software." Things can be as complex and intricate as they need to be on the inside, but at the user interface where people connect with technology, keep it as simple as possible. Not dumbed down, just simple and really clear. As Albert Einstein said, "Make everything as simple as possible—but not simpler."

Given the moves many people have made toward voluntary simplicity, it's not a shock that a Zipcar-owned Prius now symbolizes responsible car use. Not surprisingly, in 2011, Germany's Daimler decided to cut its ultra-luxury Maybach marque, a venerable and historic brand that was revived during the boom years. Daimler was only selling around 200 Maybachs a year recently, which is maybe not surprising given that this heavy sedan had a half-million dollar base price and lacked the pizzazz of sportier cars. In the Maybach category was a recent snippet I caught in the *Financial Times*, based on a report from Helsinki-based ship and energy power-plant maker Wärtsilä, seemingly a throwback to an earlier era of easy money and conspicuous consumption: "For luxury megayacht designer Stefano Pastrovich, the pursuit of simplicity is the name of the game." I don't know about you, but I'm not sure that simplicity and luxury megayacht go together anymore, if they ever did.

Don't get me wrong: Some luxury goods are actually very sustainable and eco-friendly, as they are truly built to last and to be used and handed down indefinitely—even for generations. Though pricey to begin with, a good Hermès scarf or Patek Philippe watch should, if properly cared for, last long enough to be put into the original owner's last will

> *Things can be as complex and intricate as they need to be on the inside, but at the user interface where people connect with technology, keep it as simple as possible. . . . As Albert Einstein said, "Make everything as simple as possible—but not simpler."*

and testament. In many cases, such hand-crafted goods will hold their value over time or, with some vintage versions, even increase in value given their rarity. They are the ultimate opposites of today's wasteful, disposable, throwaway consumer goods. Not that they are affordable to most, of course.

As for those who can actually afford to wear a Patek or Breguet watch that costs about as much as a decent car, I should note that even some very rich people have now embraced voluntary simplicity: Billionaire investor Nicolas Berggruen barely owns anything more than the clothes on his back (though he does stay in some nice hotels). Late, legendary, Bahamas-based equity market investor Sir John Templeton, an American original who grew up in Winchester, Tennessee with four Scottish grandparents, was famously frugal: Into his nineties, he sent his own faxes and drove a cheap Kia around Nassau, where he owned one house. He said he bought it as a value investment, given that prime oceanfront land is finite. However, word on Wall Street was that, with his inimitable foresight, he was an early investor in self-storage companies, knowing human nature and the spending habits of the American consumer.

Maybe an even more extreme example is the life of renowned executive coach Ram Charan, adviser to the CEOs of a large chunk of the Fortune 500. Not only doesn't Ram own a car (he never learned to drive), until relatively recently he didn't have any fixed abode at all. He became famous not only for his advice and clientele, but also for traveling the world on business 365 days a year and living in hotels. As needed, his small staff would FedEx to his next hotel stop a box of clean clothes and other sundries; Ram would then FedEx back his dirty laundry, which would meet him again, cleaned and folded, at his next destination.

Therein lies some of the paradox of these shifting attitudes: Some are lightening their load of possessions, but they are flying (and FedEx-ing) more. Another related trend is the way in which Italy's Slow Food movement has gone global, encouraging the idea that friends and families should slow down, power off their electronic devices, and enjoy one another's company over fresh, wholesome, locally-sourced food that is properly and lovingly cooked—with a generous glass of red wine in hand. An early figure in Slow Food was French baker Lionel Poilâne, whose obsessive perfectionism created the most amazing breads, hand-crafted from the best local ingredients. However, during the Internet bubble, Poilâne did a robust mail-order-type business, extravagantly FedExing loaves of bread from Paris to Silicon Valley at eye-popping prices. Though a pioneer of Slow Food, he lived life at a twenty-first century speed, and was unfortunately killed when his helicopter crashed off the coast of Brittany in 2002.

The key is not to avoid modernity, but to identify and eliminate the unnecessary complexity that frequently accompanies it. Seek out tools and trends in the modern context that enhance simplicity, sustainability, and self-fulfillment. Avoid, eliminate, or minimize those that do not. For businesses, this means first being clear about strategic intent, and then being ruthless about only adopting products, processes, and systems that support that strategy, rather than confusing or distracting from it. This will mean difficult decisions and not being able to satisfy all segments or all interests, but as so many companies have found in the past, trying to be everything to everyone frequently results in being nobody to no one.

But understanding which opportunities are promising from a 3-S perspective requires both foresight and peripheral vision. Most importantly, it also takes the courage to act when an inflection point is reached. As a Dutch friend of mine is fond of saying: "If you see the writing on the wall, read it." Or as the (somewhat more eloquent) late U.S. Supreme Court Justice Oliver Wendell Holmes is reported to have said, "I would not give a fig for the simplicity this side of complexity, but I would give my life for the simplicity on the other side of complexity."

Chapter 5

Repair Your Social Fabric

Why Relationships Always Trump Transactions

Spending money we don't have for things we don't need is a bad foundation for an economy or a family. It's time to stop keeping up with the Joneses and start making sure the Joneses are okay. The values of commercials and billboards are not the things we want to teach our children. Care for the poor is not just a moral duty but is critical for the common good.

—Jim Wallis, theologian, author, and CEO of Sojourners

Our success . . . will depend upon the essential rightness of the advice we give and our capacity for convincing those in authority that it is good.

—Andrew Thomas "Tom" Kearney,
late founder of A.T. Kearney

Enjoying unhurried, undistracted time with family, friends, colleagues, clients, and customers is never time wasted—on the contrary, it's absolutely essential to our personal and even organizational growth and well-being.
SOURCE: Datacraft/imagenavi/Getty Images.

You know it: We live in a time of broken bonds. The trust between employee and employer, borrower and lender, citizen and politician, consumer and manufacturer, has been eroding, or is badly damaged—and we all see and feel the consequences. When giant but besieged Swiss bank UBS recently marked its 150th anniversary, the mood was penitential. UBS Chairman Kaspar Villiger, son of a cigar manufacturer and onetime president of the Swiss Confederation, said that trust "cannot be tied to a far-dated founding year, trust constantly has to be won anew. . . . Reputation is the most important capital for a bank. It takes just a thoughtless action to lose it and the sweat of thousands to rebuild it."

The financial crisis has definitely hastened this trend, with the bellwether Edelman Trust Barometer reporting that in 2011, for the first time, there are more countries that fall under the heading of skeptics than trusting. With unemployment high and so many companies choosing to protect their bottom line through headcount reductions and productivity enhancement drives (which usually mean getting more out of each employee without paying them more), it's no wonder that employees are increasingly distrustful of employers. The failure of elected leaders to meet the challenges facing their citizens, and the perception that these same politicians are distant or immune from the problems facing the populace, has have added to a level of distrust that already existed between citizens and governments.

Much of this predated the crisis, but there is no question that several trends are combining to amplify existing breaches in trust, the crisis notwithstanding. For example, the trend toward solitary, transient living, often in socially hermetic suburbs, has led

. . . the trend toward solitary, transient living, often in socially hermetic suburbs, has led to increased individual atomization, making personal contact—and the relationships that it engenders—less frequent. Growing income inequality has reduced the sense we collectively feel that we're all in it together.

to increased individual atomization, making personal contact—and the relationships that it engenders—less frequent. Growing income inequality has reduced the sense we collectively feel that we're all in it together. Francis Fukuyama has called this a reduction in the formation of social capital. Frank's definition of social capital (in his 1999 paper entitled "Social Capital and Civil Society") may be a bit heavy: "an instantiated informal norm that promotes cooperation between two or more individuals," but he is clear that its creation rests not just on a perceived bond between people, but on an "actual human relationship" (his words) that turns an opportunity for potential cooperation into the real thing.

One of my proudest moments at A.T. Kearney was when, during the height of the financial crisis, our partners came together and decided that, of all the things toward which our scarce resources could be devoted, protecting our people was the most important. Counter to the prevailing trend of employers sacrificing staff before profits, we held our team of nearly 3,000 employees together, and we have been rewarded by having one of the highest levels of esprit de corps in our industry.

And you can't repair the bonds or rebuild relationships by sitting at your desk, so American Airlines' campaign is right: "We know why you fly." (British Airways has also caught on, and offers a contest for small business owners to win airfare to in-person meetings under its Face-to-Face promotion.) Every videoconference I participate in always seems to end with this question: When can we schedule an in-person meeting? When Turkish/American dynamo Muhtar Kent became Chairman and CEO of Coca-Cola in 2008, he said, "We had become ingrown. Most of the meetings we were holding were just with ourselves. We weren't going out to see how the world was changing." He quickly changed all that at Coke, much to the benefit of the company and its shareholders and stakeholders around the world. When it comes to the primacy of trusting relationships, Coke is at the top of its game, having a long legacy of handshake relationships fundamental to its extraordinary success. As Muhtar says in his own words, "A brand is a promise, and a good brand is a promise kept"; in

> *We had become ingrown. Most of the meetings we were holding were just with ourselves. We weren't going out to see how the world was changing.*
> *—Muhtar Kent, Chairman and CEO of Coca-Cola*

the case of Coke, those promises delivered on go well beyond the circles of consumers, shareholders, and employees, to stakeholders in nearly every country on the planet.

Relationships matter in every industry and field of human endeavor, not least in politics. I recently spoke with a former colleague on Capitol Hill, and he reminded me why the rough-and-tumble of politics seemed more substantive and less personal in years gone by. Did you know that such fierce opponents as (then) Republican Senator Dan Quayle and Democratic House Majority Leader Dick Gephardt used to commute together into Washington, braving the heavy traffic each day? It was not time wasted, as it fostered a friendly personal relationship between those—and countless others—who might otherwise disagree on most things.

In addition to engaging one another on an individual, in-person level less often, we are also allowing our virtual relationships to interfere with our tangible ones. I recently met with a Brazilian executive who said that each morning he had breakfast with at least 50 people. Astonished at what must be an enormous household, I asked how this was possible. He went on to explain that each morning the crowd at the breakfast table included himself, his wife, his two teenage daughters, and the scores of friends they were furtively texting rather than engaging in family conversation. After he put it that way, it occurred to me that I've often had family meals with a rather large number of people myself.

Toyota runs an entertaining advertisement on U.S. television that features a young woman sitting behind a laptop bemoaning the fact that she only recently convinced her parents to join Facebook. And despite her good offices they still only have a small number of Facebook friends. As she continues to explain that "this"—meaning her Facebook connection—"is living," the screen is interspersed with footage of her parents (driving a Toyota product) engaged in a number of rewarding real-life activities. Humor or preconceptions aside, we should be clear that the younger generation is not the only group at fault here—we're all guilty of leaving our BlackBerries or iPhones on a little too often.

Back to the frayed relationships (and nerves) in the political realm, one of the U.S. Congress's rising Democratic stars (and a lifelong friend) is Gerry Connolly, the former chairman of the Fairfax County Board of Supervisors in Northern Virginia (a county that, based on size, would make it the nation's thirteenth largest city, twelfth largest school district, and sixth largest office market). He argues that our tortured politics are a reflection of what's happening in the real world: "Our politics are more striated, polarized because the rewards and punishments in place penalize compromise." He also notes that the 2010 Supreme Court decision in *Citizens United v. the Federal Election Commission* forever changed the U.S. political landscape by removing previous limitations on independent spending for political purposes. The lethal combination of unlimited stores of single-issue campaign money and the rise of ubiquitous communications media now help ensure those who maintain party orthodoxy are rewarded and those who seek compromise on the important issues of the day are all too often punished.

As for the unlimited cash flooding into US politics as a result of that Supreme Court decision, the paradox is that political influence and access remain relatively cheap. Former Treasury Secretary and Harvard President Larry Summers was asked if a $250,000 contribution to Harvard would have gotten the giver a meeting with him when he was president of the university. Summers' reply: "Not a chance." But when asked what access that same amount of money would get you in Washington, he said, "You can get a meeting with the Senate Majority Leader, the Speaker of the House, the President—anyone."

Former moderate Republican Senator Arlen Specter's new book title pretty much says it all: *Life Among the Cannibals: A Political Career, A Tea Party Uprising, and the End of Government as We Know It*. It's filled with amusing anecdotes from his long political career. Less funny is his account of the increasingly frenzied take-no-prisoners atmosphere of Congress, where compromise has become a dirty word and moderates of both parties are regularly roughed up.

The Three-Line Whip

The British have developed colorful language for this kind of punishment/enforcement system drawn from the sport of fox hunting (now illegal in the UK): In Parliament, a party's one-line whip urges voting a particular way, a two-line whip requires it, and a three-line whip provides for truly draconian punishments, including expulsion, in the event a member goes against the party line. Now that's what I call an atmosphere of friendly collaboration.

Personal bonds of trust are not only essential to good politics, they also are the glue of good business. And to rebuild this sense of common purpose and community within a for-profit company, people need to spend time together just as much as they do anywhere else. Herein lies a paradox: To be effective and creative, people need time to unplug and recharge; at the same time, new sights, sounds, and human interactions can help stimulate and refresh one's thinking. As strategist Gary Hamel puts it in his book *Leading the Revolution*, "Familiarity is the enemy.

Herein lies a paradox: To be effective and creative, people need time to unplug and recharge; at the same time, new sights, sounds, and human interactions can help stimulate and refresh one's thinking.

It slowly turns everything to wallpaper. Travel makes you a stranger. It puts you at odds. It robs you of your prejudices." That team-building trip to Alaska you considered doing wasn't so wasteful after all.

There is a broader point to be made here as well: Expanding or re-engaging your (real, tangible) personal connections not only gives you an opportunity to create more shared time and experiences on which relationships are based, it's also the chance to broaden the scope of informational inputs around which one's worldview is based. I recently met, in my office in Washington, with a senior official from the Singapore government's strategy office (yes, in Singapore they have a strategy office). When I asked what other business had brought him to Washington, he replied that he periodically took trips around the world, always stopping in different cities, simply to meet with cool people (his words, I assure you, not mine) and gain their perspectives on different topics. It was his way of escaping the groupthink that can come with the same office and colleagues, day in and day out. Even more impressively, he brought his staff with him, explaining that his was not the only perspective that needed to benefit from broadening.

The Pause Principle

Kevin Cashman, the Korn/Ferry senior partner and author of *The Pause Principle* I cited earlier in the book, speaks about the way in which creative pauses are an absolutely essential ingredient to clearer leadership thinking and renewed relationships within and outside one's organization. According to Kevin, "Management effectiveness involves doing more with greater efficiency and speed, while leadership effectiveness involves doing [things] differently by slowing down to transform complexity to clarity. . . . Managers assert drive and control to get things done; leaders pause to discover new ways of being and achieving." In good consulting style, he has sketched out this very helpful two-by-two matrix:

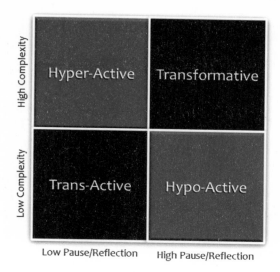

SOURCE: Courtesy of Kevin Cashman.

I think Kevin really gets it right. Low complexity combined with little reflection represents a merely repetitive, transactional environment, but things (as we know) are getting more complicated by the minute; high complexity with little reflection means being literally hyperactive, the increasingly common (and not actually productive) state of being in perpetual motion—the well-known action-hero persona. Of course too much reflection can mean being hypoactive, all thought and no action. But today's incredibly complex business and policy situations demand of us an adequate level of pause and reflection if we want to be truly transformative. As the sign used to say in every IBM building around the world, "Think."

But we all know you can't think straight if you're not feeling well, and that brings us back to the old Latin saying *mens sana in corpore sano*—a sound mind in a healthy body. That doesn't mean hitting the gym for three hours a day. It's more about finding the right balance, and it's precisely that balance which is proving so elusive in our action-packed era. It also means eating right, and our ancestors would be shocked that our problem is, increasingly, eating too much, rather than

*Management effective-
ness involves doing more
with greater efficiency
and speed, while leader-
ship effectiveness
involves doing [things]
differently by slowing
down to transform
complexity to clarity.
. . . Managers assert
drive and control to get
things done; leaders
pause to discover new
ways of being and
achieving.*
        —*Kevin Cashman*

the historic human challenge of trying to get enough to eat. As George Orwell wrote in the late 1930s, "A millionaire may enjoy breakfasting off orange juice and Ryvita biscuits; an unemployed man doesn't . . . [He wants something] a little bit 'tasty' . . ." This divergence between the lean and fit rich and the overweight poor has, if anything, widened since Orwell's time, with the easy availability of low-priced fast foods that satiate our cravings for fat, salt, and sugar.

In all this, Switzerland and its Alpine neighbors may turn out to be remembered less for their banking secrecy and more for their attention to health and wellness in their broadest sense. Switzerland, which was actually a relatively poor country for most of its 700-year history (its main export was mercenary soldiers, something that still survives in the Pope's Swiss Guard), managed to develop a strong tourist trade in the late 1800s. People came to the Alps to walk, hike, rest, ski, breathe the fresh air, and eat early health foods (like Bircher-Muesli, invented in 1900 by Swiss physician Dr. Max Bircher).

Tuberculosis patients used to go to high-altitude resort-hospital towns like Davos to dry out their lungs. The now world-famous Belvédère Hotel in Davos, mobbed by CEOs and world leaders each January, was originally a sanatorium for the well-to-do. In 1931, the La Prairie Clinic was founded on Lake Geneva in Montreux, and this institution and others like it attracted patients who wanted a more personal and holistic approach than was offered at the time by such great pinnacles of medicine as Johns Hopkins and the Mayo Clinic in America. Davos, of course, was also the setting of Thomas Mann's masterpiece *The Magic Mountain*—although the magic that goes on there these days is of a rather different sort. But even the founder of the World Economic Forum, Professor Klaus Schwab, somehow manages to find the time to be a super-fit cross-country ski marathoner. (Some have observed that Klaus had one really good idea early on and has run with it ever since. That kind of remark suggests sour grapes, as few of us ever have one idea in our lifetimes as good as the Davos meeting idea, and even fewer can execute it with as much panache and success as Klaus has.)

This Alpine tradition of healthful balance has carried over to our day, where it is needed more than ever. Not surprisingly, Nestlé, the world's largest food company—headquartered in the quaint lakeside resort town of Vevey—has remade itself as the world's leading wellness company (as I will tell you more about in the next chapter). If you are fortunate to visit Nestlé's corporate headquarters on a clear, sunny day, the view from the lobby is spectacular—and the food in the employee cafeteria (or canteen) is superb and fitness-focused. On a coffee table, you might spy a copy of *The Alpine Diet*, a book by an American cardiologist who has practiced nearby for several decades. On the other side of the country, down-to-earth cement billionaire, philanthropist, and investor Thomas Schmidheiny has turned his family-developed Grand Resort Bad Ragaz into the best well-being, medical health, and thermal spa in the world. You have to see it to believe it, and your mind and body will thank you. It's a nineteenth century ideal fully updated for the twenty-first.

All in the Family

Of course one can't speak of renewing relationships without touching on those all-important family relationships. Most businesses around the world are still family businesses. In fact, I would say that the evolution of (and even revolution in) the family-owned enterprise is one of the megatrends of our time. In Asia, Latin America, and the Middle East, most large companies remain family-owned, or at least family-controlled—and in these regions of the world, trust is primarily built on family relationships.

Of course one can't speak of renewing relationships without touching on those all-important family relationships. Most businesses around the world are still family businesses. In fact, I would say that the evolution of (and even revolution in) the family-owned enterprise is one of the megatrends of our time.

If we look at older family-controlled companies in North America and Europe that have continued to grow and prosper for decades, even centuries, you will note several things: While the family imprint is still very much there, management talent is mostly brought in from the outside. Families that want to see their fortunes grow see their role as keepers of the flame—as chairmen and board members, permanent sources of capital, guardians of continuity and cultural DNA, but also as hard-working talent scouts for people and ideas that come from the outside. You will find relatively few (or in some cases any) family owners among the management ranks these days in such privately-held giants as Cargill, Bechtel, or Mars (the candy people)—or in such publicly-traded companies with key family shareholdings as Molson Coors, where seventh-generation Canadian brewer Andrew Molson became chairman in 2011 in succession to Pete Coors of Golden, Colorado.

Absent direct market pressures, family companies can get sleepy—and eventually lose the passion and creativity that they were known for in their founding years. But there is no rule that says that family enterprises need to follow that life cycle from early energetic growth to greatness to eventual decline and sale or breakup. Just look at BMW, where an intense performance orientation (in every sense) remains in place not despite family control but arguably because of it. The low-key Quandt family retains its near-50 percent (direct and indirect) ownership of BMW, and a 40-something Stefan Quandt, who had a succession of real jobs outside the company (from Minneapolis to Hong Kong), maintains a quiet but committed family presence on the BMW supervisory board.

Sometimes the family imprint is maintained in other ways: The world's largest auto parts maker, Robert Bosch of Stuttgart, Germany, is renowned for its exacting precision engineering, but it is now 92 percent owned by the Robert Bosch Foundation, which is both a grant-making and an operating foundation running its own programs (including a notable fellowship program for young American professionals who want to spend a year working in Germany). Likewise, the Wallenberg family—the Rockefellers of Sweden—have vested much of their shareholdings in their multiple family foundations, which in turn control the publicly traded Investor AB holding company that has large stakes in such major global companies as ABB, Electrolux, AstraZeneca, and Ericsson. (This also shows that, more than ever, the boundaries between public, private, for-profit, non-profit, and even state-owned have gotten quite blurred—a trend that I think is going to accelerate in the future.)

But I'll admit it's hard to keep going from generation to generation, even when the cultural DNA is distinctive. You may know that Britain was once home to a number of major companies that were founded by Quaker families, including Cadbury, Rowntree, Carr's (biscuits), Fry's (chocolate)—even Barclays Bank. The emphasis on chocolate (for drinking and eating) was part of the Quaker social conscience, in order to give consumers a temperance alternative to gin and the like. But this Quaker legacy is today a footnote to history, and none of these storied firms has remained in family hands—and most were bought by other companies.

It all comes back to relationships. Where they thin out, watch out. Where they remain strong, the underlying enterprise remains intact and growing. C. Hoare & Co., the discreet multibillion-pound private bank based on London's Fleet Street, was founded in 1672 and is still going strong in its eleventh generation of family ownership. You might not know its name, but by some measures, it's the most successful UK financial institution, and it saw large inflows of assets during the recent financial crisis. You know what? The partners still sit together in the same room (literally—with a group of desks in the partners' room), and the partners still have a good lunch together every day (when not out with clients). No wonder they're still in business after almost 350 years.

Chapter 6

Don't Wait for the Next Big Thing

If I'd asked people what they wanted, they would have said a faster horse.

—Henry Ford

The future's already arrived. It's just not evenly distributed yet.
—Paul Saffo, technology forecaster and board member, The Long Now Foundation, quoting novelist William Gibson

Why didn't the flying car ever "take off"? There is nothing wrong with day-dreaming about possible innovations, but if we're obsessed with quantum leaps inspired by science fiction, we're missing the point.
SOURCE: Corbis.

If you're trying to come up with the next big thing, don't ask your customers—they can't tell you—even though conventional wisdom says you should begin with market research. Thanks to the Internet and other innovations, power (including pricing power) has shifted to consumers, who are increasingly the co-creators of the products and services they buy—and a certain level of customer engagement is indeed necessary in a highly interconnected world. However, companies need to avoid being continually reactive; successful companies of the future will be those that surprise and delight their customers—something the world came to expect from Steve Jobs.

And if you are simply treading water and waiting for the next big thing or next big boom, think again. Remember that old bumper sticker: "Please Lord, just one more boom—I promise not to blow it this time"? If you are longing for the good old days of easy leverage, steadily rising asset prices, cheap natural resources, and that sleight-of-hand of lower taxes and higher government expenditures. . . . Forget it. Just wake up and get on with innovating—seizing smaller opportunities in the absence of clear macro signals. The companies and governments that are successful in doing so will be those that are open to the broadest range of inputs and have a sufficiently flexible view of the world going forward to interpret them. But you can't have capitalism without capitalists, and I've often thought that, much as we have portable, tax-advantaged IRAs (individual retirement accounts) in the United States and similar vehicles in other countries, governments should create the possibility for analogous accounts that people can tap for lifelong education and re-training expenses as well as for start-up capital for small businesses.

Sometimes a humble innovation turns out to be world changing, and I think an example of such a relatively unsung innovation is the standardized shipping container invented in the 1950s. Containerized shipping forever changed the world by making the transport of goods far cheaper and enormously more efficient.

Sometimes a humble innovation turns out to be world changing, and I think an example of such a relatively unsung innovation is the standardized shipping container invented in the 1950s. Containerized shipping forever changed the world by making the transport of goods far cheaper and enormously more efficient. But you won't find too many odes or ballads dedicated to it.

When, for example, you are the world's largest food company—Nestlé, with well over a $100 billion in worldwide sales—it's hard to find any trend or strategy large enough to move the needle. But that is just what they are doing in powering sales growth with a number of smaller new innovations, including those incorporating health and wellness benefits without compromising taste—what some call functional food, at the nexus where nutrition and pharma meet. Under the leadership of Austrian-born Peter Brabeck, this Swiss-based giant has repositioned itself at least partially (and very profitably) as a health and wellness company. Peter, now Nestlé's chairman, says, "We have to move to personalized nutrition and, through it, to personalized preventative health programs," and his very able successor as CEO, Paul Bulcke, is making it happen. Yes, Nestlé will continue to sell you everything from their dazzling array of brands, from San Pellegrino water and Häagen-Dazs ice cream to KitKats, Nescafé, Purina Friskies, Buitoni pasta, Gerber baby food, Stouffer's frozen meals, and the Nespresso single-serving quality coffee machine, to mention only a tiny fraction of what they sell globally. But the ingredients lists will always be evolving—for the better.

Nestlé has even teamed up with the Institute for Snow and Avalanche Research in Switzerland to study microscopic ice crystals in the hope of making even better ice cream. "Ice cream is an inherently unstable substance . . . the ice will separate from the original ingredients such as cream and sugar," says Dr. Hans Jörg Limbach, a scientist at the Nestlé Research Center. I knew that some explosives were inherently unstable, but ice cream—who knew? Anyway, Nestlé is hot on the case. Nestlé, of course, is a leader in many areas of food innovation, both in terms of health and nutrition but also sustainability, and has a team of over 5,000 professionals working across 32 different research centers to deliver on their corporate commitment to create what Peter calls "shared value."

Now, some do question whether even this level of innovation is fast enough or simply big enough to make a real difference to the world. Such serious analysts of the business environment as billionaire venture capitalist Peter Thiel and economist Tyler Cowen believe that innovation has actually plateaued for several years. They make the point that it's not a question of ever-rising patent numbers, but rather the apparent slowdown in the creation of profoundly breakthrough technologies that increase standards of living and change the way life is lived (beyond those related to the Internet). My blue-collar father made a similar point late in his life in 1990, saying, "Son, the changes you will see in your lifetime can't possibly be bigger than the ones I saw in my lifetime—the ability of ordinary families to have cars, TVs, and travel by jet . . . the fact we no longer worry about kids getting polio thanks to the Salk vaccine . . . and now we've got the fax machine and the computer. How could the pace of change get any more amazing?"

Innovation: Slowing Down or Speeding Up? (I Think the Latter)

In the view of Peter Thiel, the signs of an innovation slowdown are everywhere if we dare to look. For the first time in recorded history, travel and transport speeds are slowing—and he notes that even the ever-shrewd Warren Buffett has made a recent $44 billion investment in the American railroad industry, which "will do especially well if transport and energy consumption patterns involve a regression to the past."

According to Thiel's measures, increases in agricultural productivity are also slowing, increases in U.S. life expectancy are decelerating, pharmaceutical industry pipelines for blockbuster drugs are looking a bit empty, companies and investors are still looking to "juice" returns with leverage rather than with productivity gains driven by scientific and technological advances—and bold dreams of progress hardly exist outside the IT sector. Though a self-described libertarian, Thiel admits,

> The state can successfully push science; there is no sense denying it. The Manhattan Project and the Apollo program remind us of this possibility. Free markets may not fund as much basic research as needed. . . . Today a letter from Einstein would get lost in the White House mail room, and the Manhattan Project would not even get started; it certainly could never be completed in three years. . . . Robert Moses, the great builder of New York City in the 1950s and 1960s, or Oscar Niemeyer, the great architect of Brasilia, belong to a past when people still had concrete ideas about the future. Voters today prefer Victorian houses. [Even] science fiction has collapsed as a literary genre.

In the other corner, we have MIT-trained inventor and entrepreneur Ray Kurzweil, who argues that science continues to advance at an explosive, accelerating rate even if much is still invisible to the naked eye—and that, by 2045, those still alive will benefit from regenerative medicine that stops and in fact reverses aging, entirely. Not that you'll need your body much beyond that, according to Ray, who expects most biological forms will merge with machine forms by then, and artificial intelligence will so far surpass the human mind that humans will no longer even grasp what's going on. It all sounds very sci-fi (and even horrifying), and it would be easier to dismiss Ray if he hadn't been so successful in developing speech recognition technology, optical character recognition systems, and other innovations long before the world thought them possible.

What Peter Thiel and Ray Kurzweil do agree on is that the IT world continues to display a vibrancy we wish we saw in all industries right now. There are even glimmers of hope that the growing information overload described earlier in the book is responding to some therapeutic technical fixes. Ever come across Tibco, a software company based in Palo Alto that works for clients ranging from Amazon to the U.S. Department of Homeland Security? As one of its executives, Murat Sonmez, explained in Davos earlier this year, their expertise is in "sifting through and finding patterns in the acceleratingly expansive universe of digital data." He continued, "We can predict when a gambler at a slot machine will cease to be happy." According to the *New Yorker* writer who interviewed him at the World Economic Forum's annual meeting, "He explained how Tibco, on behalf of Harrah's, had designed a system that can figure out when a gambler is about to encounter a loss of such magnitude that it will cause him to leave the casino and perhaps never come back."

Maybe if it works for Las Vegas, it can eventually help us?

Knowledge Hatcheries

In the meantime, we do have to live in the here and now, even as we try to build a future worth sticking around for. Ever heard of the Kansai Science City in Japan, or anything about Malaysia's Cyberjaya? You have to give the Malaysians and Japanese credit for trying to create new Silicon Valleys—from scratch. It turns out to be very difficult to do, regardless of the formula (and gobs of money) used as ingredients. Russia's Skolkovo area outside Moscow is just the latest such attempt, though the Russians are sensibly doing it in collaboration with MIT—so as to create the right kind of nutrient base for innovation.

Don Tapscott, author of *Wikinomics*, correctly says, "The future lies in collaboration across borders, cultures, companies, and disciplines. The collaboration economy offers endless possibilities for growth, innovation, and diversity." This sentiment is echoed by former P&G Chairman A. G. Lafley: "No company today, no matter how large or how global, can innovate fast enough or big enough by itself. Collaboration—externally with consumers and customers, suppliers and business partners, and internally across business and organization

Ever heard of the Kansai Science City in Japan, or anything about Malaysia's Cyberjaya? You have to give the Malaysians and Japanese credit for trying to create new Silicon Valleys—from scratch. It turns out to be very difficult to do, regardless of the formula (and gobs of money) used as ingredients.

boundaries—is critical." As I say elsewhere in this book, I truly believe that diversity and inclusion are absolutely essential ingredients of innovation, which is why A.T. Kearney is championing these values. But I need to be clear: Sometimes diversity (particularly in academic institutions) has become a slogan representing a new orthodoxy and a new monoculture. A company will not be more creative if everyone thinks (and dresses) the way Steve Jobs did; wearing a black turtleneck doesn't confer new insights on the wearer. By diversity I mean a genuine diversity of ideas and points of view, and by inclusion I have in mind the broadest possible spectrum of talented and engaged people coming from many different backgrounds, cultures, and countries. To put it simply, you won't learn all that much from people just like yourself. Or, as our founder Tom Kearney wrote "The true strength of this firm, as in any organization, lies in the fact that we are all different . . . the strength inherent in this firm rests upon these collective and diverse interests. They are all we have."

But what exactly is the secret sauce, or *je ne sais quoi*, of those clusters of creativity that actually work? Richard Florida, of Toronto's Rotman School, argues that economic vitality erupts from hip, edgy, tolerant places that make life (and careers) interesting for unconventional thinkers and doers. Los Angeles-based Joel Kotkin vehemently disagrees, saying that few cities can actually be successful catering to "wealthy cosmopolites wishing to enjoy urban amenities in the elegantly recycled shell of a former business center." Our own A.T. Kearney Global Cities Index seeks to measure the vibrancy and connectedness of a city not just by looking at economic or financial measures, but also by incorporating cultural, educational, entertainment, and other metrics. We do this because we recognize that innovation and opportunity come in a city with a full, rounded package, rather than a specific development program or incentive.

As a way of kickstarting their own post-oil futures, Abu Dhabi and Qatar have decided to invest in things other than the kind of limitless skyscraper development you have in Dubai. Don't get me wrong: Dubai has already turned itself into one of the world's great business hubs for travel (through its legendary mega-airport, roughly halfway between Europe and India), lifestyle, investment, banking, and general can-do attitude. It can justifiably claim to be the de facto business capital of the entire Middle East region. So the neighbors of Dubai, such as Abu Dhabi and Qatar, have to do something different in order to thrive on their own terms. The former has established a satellite of the world's best-loved art museum—the Louvre Abu Dhabi, and in similar Francophile tones, the latter is launching a branch campus of France's renowned Saint-Cyr military academy in Doha (to be a Middle Eastern equivalent of America's West Point and Britain's Sandhurst).

In some way, small countries have an advantage that they never used to have: In past eons, small states lived at the mercy of their mightier neighbors. Today, however, small jurisdictions can be much more nimble than bigger ones. Liechtenstein, wedged between Switzerland and Austria, has a bit of an image problem related to its banking secrecy. Fortunately, its reigning prince, Hans-Adam II, is a successful entrepreneur in his own right (developing new rice strains for a hungry Asia) and something of a one-man think tank. His new book is *The State in the Third Millennium*, and it includes new model constitutions that allow you to fill in the blank where it says Kingdom of X or Republic of Y—meant, of course, to stimulate government thinking. In the

In some way, small countries have an advantage that they never used to have: In past eons, small states lived at the mercy of their mightier neighbors. Today, however, small jurisdictions can be much more nimble than bigger ones.

meantime, his pocket-sized principality with the medieval ring to its name has adopted what is arguably the most carefully constructed (and shortest) modern constitution in the world, after appropriately fierce debate.

Philip Bobbitt, the debonair Texas-born bestselling author, constitutional lawyer, scenario planner, national security expert, and all-around Renaissance man who is sometimes called the "James Bond of Columbia Law School," makes the point that too many governments have failed to anticipate how to adapt the rule of law to future circumstances. Instead, in times of crisis, leaders have frequently looked for ways to step around, ignore, or even violate inconvenient laws—making a mockery of their oaths to uphold the law and calling into question the legitimacy of the whole system. Wouldn't it better if they thought a few steps ahead? Planning for possible mass-scale bio-terrorism, for example, Philip says, "We should stockpile laws for [a catastrophic] eventuality, just as we stockpile vaccines." Likewise, in thinking about large areas of the world where low-intensity conflict is endemic, he notes that security forces need to be more than police, but less than an army. This requires reviving a legal concept that still exists in some places—a hybrid constabulary. (Surviving examples of national constabulary forces include France's Gendarmerie, Spain's Guardia Civil, Canada's RCMP—the Mounties—and Italy's famously brave and incorruptible Carabinieri, who better than most stood up to the Mafia without flinching.)

These kinds of insights and innovations in jurisprudence are also powering another new movement, the Charter City experiment being rolled out by NYU economist Paul Romer. It's really hard to create a new Silicon Valley, but what about a new Hong Kong? The idea is that, for example, if Nigeria is an ungovernable mess, no one can possibly take on the whole country; but maybe it's possible to carve out a small area, and make sure everything works properly—from the justice system to infrastructure and education to public services and neighborhood safety.

You can watch this experiment in real time: Honduras, with its poverty and crime high even by the generally sad standards of Central America, has decided to give it a try and has formed new special development regions based on Romer's ideas. They will be new autonomous city-states, with their own laws and some foreign supervision that bypasses the Honduran central government. This may be the most interesting new urban laboratory in the world. Nearby Costa Rica shows something to reach for: Under the 1990s leadership of President José María Figueres (a West Pointer who went on to become World Economic Forum managing director), we saw Costa Rica become safe, successful, and attractive, drawing in investors, retirees, and tourists by the planeload.

In trolling for new things, one of the most important things you can do is try to identify the stereotypes you are carrying around in your mind, and be conscious of them because they create blind spots—not to mention other problems. That's why I've suggested that you constantly look for new sources of information and ideas, and not just remotely from the comfort of your desk: You need to get out into the world and see what's going on for yourself.

Honduras, with its poverty and crime high even by the generally sad standards of Central America, has decided to give it a try and has formed new special development regions based on Romer's ideas. They will be new autonomous city-states, with their own laws and some foreign supervision that bypasses the Honduran central government. This may be the most interesting new urban laboratory in the world.

A stereotype that's gotten more entrenched in recent years is the image of Muslims around the world as bomb-throwing fundamentalists. The reality is a vast arc of humanity numbering some 1.6 billion people. This arc spans the world from relatively peaceful Morocco in western North Africa all the way down to Southeast Asia to the world's most populous Islamic country—Indonesia, where radical Islamist views have never had a strong hold. In between is not only the Middle East with its well-known problems, but also the moderate world of Central Asian Islam in places like Kazakhstan. Companies that get this are not steering clear of Muslims and the Islamic world, but rather including them proactively as executives, employees, clients, and customers. Banking giant HSBC, with its cross-cultural Sino-Scottish roots in Hong Kong and Shanghai, has become one of the world's biggest players in Islamic finance through its HSBC Amanah unit. And if you visit an upscale Whole Foods Market in North America, I might suggest a detour to the frozen food aisle, where you can stock up on some frozen dinners made by Saffron Road. They are delicious, Halal-certified, all-natural, sustainably farmed, and antibiotic-free meals, and clearly appeal to non-Muslims as well as Muslims.

You won't hear much about him in headlines that these days prefer to focus on sensationalized breaking news (i.e., bad news), but there is also an imam you should know more about, who is a major force for peaceful progress, education, and economic growth across a wide swath of the Islamic world. In fact, he is trying hard to spark a renewal of the scientific creative edge that Islamic civilization was once known for (remember we use Arabic numerals, and such words as algebra and algorithm come from medieval Arabic).

You may have guessed that I'm thinking of Karim, the fourth Aga Khan and forty-ninth Imam of the Shia Ismaili Muslims. Born in Switzerland and raised there and in Nairobi, Kenya, he had originally hoped to study science at MIT—but his grandfather insisted on nearby Harvard instead. A competitive downhill skier, he skied for Iran in the 1964 Winter Olympics in Innsbruck, though given his British, French, Pakistani, and Indian links he could have skied for any number of other countries. With the death of his grandfather, he became the forty-ninth Imam at the age of 20, and immediately threw himself into a large number of investment, development, and philanthropic initiatives, from the Indian subcontinent and the Middle East to East Africa and Central Asia, all with an emphasis on bringing back peace, prosperity, and creativity to the Islamic world. The cutting-edge Aga Khan Museum, which will showcase Islamic art and culture, will open in Toronto in 2013. In the Canadian capital, Ottawa, his handsome and ultra-modern Delegation of the Ismaili Imamat functions as a kind of embassy. And if you find yourself vacationing in Italy's marvelous Costa Smeralda in northern Sardinia, you might want to note that the place was sensitively developed starting in 1961 by a young Aga Khan, then, as now, a shrewd investor.

Offer a Prize

Speaking of laboratories of innovation, here is another old idea that is now coming back into fashion: the incentive prize. Long before the rise of the modern philanthropic grant-making foundation, whose form was established by the Rockefeller and Ford families in the early twentieth century, prizes were more common than grants as methods for trying to spur innovation and solve specific problems. Most famously, in 1714 the British Parliament dangled a big-ticket cash prize for anyone who could figure out a simple and practical way for ships to determine their exact longitude—an important issue for the world's leading sea-power of the day. It took several decades, but the problem was solved, and the prize purse was distributed. In a similar way, Napoleon Bonaparte, understanding that armies march on their stomachs, offered a cash prize to anyone who developed a reliable method for preserving food. In response, after several years of experimentation, a French cook and inventor discovered how to can food safely (and got the prize money). In the 1920s, New York hotelier Raymond Orteig offered a cash prize for the first person to fly nonstop from New York to Paris (or vice versa). Charles Lindbergh, in his now-famous plane *The Spirit of St. Louis*, won the Orteig Prize in 1927 for a more than 33-hour solo transatlantic flight. Lindbergh won a cash prize of $25,000 (the equivalent of some $350,000 in today's money) and a lifetime of fame (and fame-related problems).

Long before the rise of the modern philanthropic grant-making foundation, whose form was established by the Rockefeller and Ford families in the early twentieth century, prizes were more common than grants as methods for trying to spur innovation and solve specific problems.

Today, the nerve center of this renaissance of incentive prizes is not London or Paris or New York, but rather Santa Monica, California—headquarters of the X-Prize Foundation, which is funded by the co-founders of Google, Dustin Moskovitz of Facebook fame, and other (mostly) digerati. A recent example of their incentive prizes is the Progressive Insurance Automotive X-Prize, with a $10 million purse given for the creation of super-efficient gasoline-powered vehicles that can get 100 miles or more to the gallon. Not all problems lend themselves to incentive prizes, and it frequently costs more money to be a credible contender than the value of the prize itself. Like the America's Cup, the best-designed prize competitions provide a strong incentive of glory and fame beyond the check in the envelope. For companies, the trick is to determine what makes successful examples so and to replicate them within their own corporate environments.

Not all problems lend themselves to incentive prizes, and it frequently costs more money to be a credible contender than the value of the prize itself. Like the America's Cup, the best-designed prize competitions provide a strong incentive of glory and fame beyond the check in the envelope.

The X-Prize Foundation's founder and head is Peter Diamandis, who grew up on Long Island to Greek immigrant parents and went on to earn degrees from MIT and Harvard Medical School. Paraphrasing Abraham Lincoln and Peter Drucker, Diamandis has adopted this as his personal motto: "The best way to predict the future is to create it yourself." Not a bad idea.

Diamandis is, in fact, following his own advice, having cofounded a venture called Planetary Resources. The company, which is also backed by Google co-founder Larry Page and filmmaker James Cameron, aims to address critical resource shortages by launching unmanned spacecraft to mine near-earth asteroids (Cameron, of course, has some experience with advanced robotic vehicles from some of his deep-water films, and offered advice to BP during the Macondo well leak).

As businesses nimbly innovate and create their own futures, they need to be able to find talent that is up to this challenge. In his new book *The Start-up of You*, Reid Hoffman, cofounder of the professional networking site LinkedIn, recommends that individuals treat their careers as though they were a one-person start-up. Start-ups, the argument goes, are forced by necessity into being highly responsive, highly innovative, and constantly ahead of the curve. Further, they are willing (and compelled) to take intelligent risks, to invest in themselves, and to network with other similarly situated organizations. Hoffman's view is that in a constantly changing, high-speed world, the characteristics that make start-ups successful are also necessary for personal career success.

Innovation has become something of a watchword in the popular business press, recently making the cover of a special issue of the *Harvard Business Review*. Given all the attention that this topic has received, why is it that companies, governments, and individuals still have such a difficult time just innovating? Even given the organizational and structural constraints (and solutions) discussed previously, why do leaders so frequently fail to drive innovation or recognize an innovation when one is presented to them?

There are three key causes: They can't process the general information overload of the modern business context and are thus unable to filter out quality opportunities in a specific context; they lack the peripheral vision to sense unidentified trends or weak signals that point to innovative opportunities, and are left unimpressed today by tomorrow's hit idea; and finally, they lack what nineteenth century American philosopher William James described as the "will to believe"—that is, the will to take decisive action in the face of uncertainty.

James' school, the philosophical pragmatists, argued against the quest for absolute truth and certainty if that quest had the effect of limiting or short-circuiting action. In the view of the pragmatists, it was a far better thing to take action and be wrong than to continue to search for certainty while delaying, or taking no action. A hallmark of some of the most innovative places in the world has been a tradition of risk-taking, perhaps most famously in California's Silicon Valley, where having started and failed at a business is almost a badge of honor.

It's no surprise that of the $28.4 billion invested in 3,673 deals by venture capital funds in 2011, Silicon Valley was the most favored destination, receiving nearly 6.5 times as much investment as the next-closest competitor, New York. Despite the rise of so-called Silicon Alley, when venture groups are searching for the next Google or Facebook to fund, even at the very earliest stages, Northern California is still the first stop.

But there are concerns that the risk tolerance of early-stage investors is decreasing in the wake of the financial crisis, and the types of projects are in less revolutionary spaces than in times past. There are further concerns that these new ventures may not be able to deliver on the social promises of job creation that are needed to help pull the global economy—particularly in the developed world—out of its funk. At a recent debate on innovation sponsored by *The Economist*, participants were asked to consider the proposition that "America is winning the innovation race." I was struck by how quickly the debate turned into an America versus China discussion, with the con side stressing the investments in basic research and infrastructure that China is making but that the United States (and many other developed nations) are not. The pro side countered that, no matter how much China spent, the innovative culture of the United States, and in particular Silicon Valley, would always have answers.

The audience was fairly evenly split on which side had the more persuasive position, but something struck me about the con position. While their side essentially conceded the point that the United States was, from a culture and human capital perspective, uniquely positioned to remain highly innovative, they countered that most of the successful recent innovations coming out of the United States were in the IT space, with the remainder commercialized elsewhere. The claim was that these ventures are inherently limited in their job-generating potential. Facebook and Twitter, the argument continued, are playing in a space where government support is not needed (or, really, has already been provided in the form of late Cold War-era DARPA research that resulted in the Internet), and have limited personnel needs. By contrast, start-ups in the renewable energy and biotech spaces have greater job-creation potential, but without the proper supports cannot attract the capital to get off the ground in this country.

Of course, none of these positions is wrong, and all get at a piece of the truth. An innovative economy requires smart government policies and investment, a risk-taking private sector, and a culture of diversity and inclusion. Unconstrained by the rules of an Oxford-style debate, I'm not going to place a bet here on specific geography or location. What I will say is that those countries, regions, and cities that manage to mix the right cocktail of policy, risk-taking, culture, diversity, and—importantly—cash will be the innovation hubs of the future, and those that miss one or more of these crucial ingredients will be left behind.

How do you—as a business leader or policy-maker—get this cocktail right? The answer has to be clear, effective, values-based leadership that

- Identifies the challenge correctly.
- Properly incentivizes risk-taking.
- Drives diversity of ideas and inclusion of people at all levels.
- Is decisive enough to take concrete, targeted action.

A. G. Lafley, the former P&G chairman I referenced earlier, penned a memorable article in *Harvard Business Review*'s May 2009 issue in which he made a similar point. Titled "What Only the CEO Can Do," Lafley outlined the elements of a business idea that can only come from leadership—and must come from leadership in order for an organization to be successful. In Lafley's view, these four things are:

- Defining the Meaningful Outside—determining, of all your external stakeholders, which are the most important.
- Deciding What Business You Are In—where should you play to win, and where should you not play at all?
- Balancing Present and Future—defining realistic growth goals that establish credibility in the short run while also keeping one eye firmly trained on the future.
- Shaping Values and Standards—values establish a company's identity. This may be dismissed by some as the softest of these four

CEO-level tasks, but they are truly among the most important. Without standards and values, a company is rudderless and cannot successfully reach its goals; it is unable to inspire and align its stakeholders, failing to drive passion around a bigger purpose.

The point here, again, is that in order for a public or private organization to be successful there has to be a clear vision that sets direction while not losing sight of the outside world or the long term. A clear, compelling vision is what motivates the people in an organization to action (remember the words of American writer Ralph Waldo Emerson: "Nothing great was ever achieved without enthusiasm"). This vision can only be delivered through leadership that is driven by a set of values and principles that are clearly, consistently, and compellingly communicated and observed.

Fighting Complexity with Complexity

Earlier in the book, I mentioned how the Santa Fe Institute is leading the way in helping us understand complexity so that we can regain at least some mastery over it. To give you an example, diseases can now spread from one part of the world to another in a matter of hours, as we saw in the deadly SARS outbreak that gripped Toronto (and the world) in 2003, thanks to a sick airline passenger who arrived there from China. While we are still far from able to instantaneously address new developments that crop up, thanks to the world's hyperconnectedness, the same technologies and connections that transmit disturbances at high speed from one place to another are already being harnessed to monitor potential dangers in real time. In the next one to two decades, expect to see companies, governments, public health authorities, and other organizations turn complexity to their advantage, as big data (that is, data sets that exceed the capabilities of traditional analytics tools and technologies, currently greater than 1 terabyte) will be monitored, analyzed, and responded to in real time.

As Santa Fe Institute researchers recently explained in Davos, "Complexity theory is giving new insights into how to protect computer systems from malicious agents, using ideas from immunology, epidemiology, and ecology. In nature, there is an ever-raging arms race between attackers and defenders, with the constant evolution of weapons and defense. . . . [Fortunately] the control of a complex system need not mean the control of all its individual elements. [For example,] the complex wiring of a car is controlled by [only] three control points: the steering wheel, gas pedal, and brake. Each one activates thousands of other components the driver is not aware of."

Brian Arthur, an Irish-born economist, technologist, and former Stanford professor who helped found SFI, has spent a lifetime studying the deep changes in the economy and society wrought by technological change. In Brian's view, we are in the midst of a profound set of transformations charac-

In the next one to two decades, expect to see companies, governments, public health authorities, and other organizations turn complexity to their advantage, as big data (that is, data sets that exceed the capabilities of traditional analytics tools and technologies, currently greater than 1 terabyte) will be monitored, analyzed, and responded to in real time.

terized by hyper-connectivity, digitization, and growing complexity. If everything is connected to everything else, both good and bad things propagate at warp speed. You may remember that in the early 1990s, technology commentator George Gilder and Ethernet co-founder Robert Metcalfe proposed that the value or power of a network is proportional to the square of the number of users (i.e., users^2)—which became known as Metcalfe's Law. Although some researchers say that this computation is merely notional and not literally true, there is no doubt that the network effects of today's hyper-connectivity are very potent indeed.

By digitization, Brian means something very specific. He's referring to the unseen economy beneath the surface of life that is teeming with processes triggering other processes: servers talking to other servers, with a vast array of technologies doing the work, from lasers and photonics to satellites—for example, when you perform the simple act of swiping your credit card at an airport check-in kiosk. While daily life may in some respects seem relatively unchanged from 10 or 20 years ago, apart from the obvious (like your ability to read this book on an iPad), the reality is actually more dramatic, if largely invisible to the naked eye. As with most dramatic changes in history, great wealth creation and business opportunity come with the elimination of entire job categories—from telephone operators, mail sorters, and airplane navigators to bookstore owners, typists, and bookkeepers, to name only a few occupations that are already mostly history.

As Brian puts it in one of his recent journal articles, "This second [unseen] economy isn't producing anything tangible. It's not making my bed in a hotel or bringing me orange juice in the morning. But it is running an awful lot of the economy." Whole new industries are coming into being, the economy is re-forming based on new engines of growth, and—as always—human institutions are barely keeping up with what is happening, and it will take governments and societies quite a while to catch up and indeed catch their breath. Like it or not, the entire world has become an "evolving complex system" that is "self-organizing" but not yet "self-healing"—"automatic and neurally intelligent, with no upper limit to its buildout. . . . This second economy that is silently forming—vast, interconnected, and extraordinarily productive—is creating for us a new economic world. How we will fare in this world, how we will adapt to it, how we will profit from and share its benefits, is very much up to us."

> *This second [unseen] economy isn't producing anything tangible. It's not making my bed in a hotel or bringing me orange juice in the morning. But it is running an awful lot of the economy.*
>
> *—Brian Arthur*

Coming Soon: Information Overload, Tamed and Ready to Serve You?

In fact, we are already making headway in this field at A.T. Kearney by pioneering new methods of big data analysis, predictive analytics, and data visualization—so that we can all shovel out from the data blizzard. The details in each of these are, as you might imagine, highly complex (explaining, for example, a technique known as massively parallel processing could potentially require a separate book), and we're fortunate to have some extremely bright minds on the case. But the essential element in what we're doing is to use technology to solve a problem seemingly created by technology. The terabyte (or multi-terabyte) data sets that technology has enabled companies to capture only add confusion, paralysis, and cost without the right tools to understand them. Rather than adding layers to that complexity through endless (but not more usable) analysis or, worse yet, ignoring large parts of the available data in an attempt at faux simplicity, our focus has been to harness the data and make it understandable, intuitive, and most importantly, actionable.

As we neared the turn of the twentieth century, it seemed as though every corporate IT department on earth was obsessed with avoiding disaster—the now mostly forgotten Y2K scare. Once it was apparent that the world as we knew it would not come to an end on January 1, 2000, they refocused on implementing corporate-wide systems to improve data availability and accuracy. As these systems came online (often very late and significantly over budget), data availability seemed to increase exponentially—and then the issue became how to digest it all.

Although Moore's Law (stating that computing power doubles approximately every two years) appears to be holding (for now), it has not resulted in diminishing this challenge—on the contrary. In fact, we are finding problems to solve as well as opportunities to pursue at Fortune 500 firms that require slicing and dicing terabytes or more of data. Without new approaches, making effective use of data becomes intractable on every dimension—running a single analysis could take a week even on a powerful computer, developing and testing a model could take a year or more, and presenting the results in a format that is intelligible to human beings is beyond the capabilities of the ubiquitous PowerPoint-type application.

All is not lost, however, as companies are finding ways to tackle these issues. Specifically, my firm is working intensively to address these distinct but related dimensions:

- **Big Data:** A catch-all term that refers to handling, processing, and analyzing data sets that are too big (more than a terabyte given today's technology) for traditional relational database tools and techniques. This means that companies may have large sets of data that they are unable to efficiently process. By comparison, big data systems are built to process data well in excess of a terabyte in essentially real time, or nearly so. With the emergence of analytics-based decision modeling (or predictive analytics or advanced analytics), the ability to process these large volumes of data quickly can provide a competitive advantage by tightening the feedback loop between customer and provider. The most visible technology supporting these big data efforts is known as massively parallel processing (MPP). MPP is a set of distributed computers, integrated in a way that supports parallel data processing. Basically, companies are taking advantage of new tools that allow MPP, along with a distributed data model, to effectively attack many terabytes of data.

- **Predicative Analytics:** A way of analyzing and modeling data to predict outcomes that result in clear actionable tasks. It requires building fast-running algorithms that are executed against large data sets. Predictive analytics is frequently used in conjunction with customer relationship management (CRM) systems and in support of marketing campaigns. A CRM system will house (theoretically) all interactions between a business and its consumers. The value lies in the ability to quickly mine this data and predict what offers, products, and services are relevant to a particular subset of customers. This segmentation permits focus on customers who are more likely to respond to the product, service, or offer.

As with Big Data, the ability to provide predictive analyses in real time is what makes these techniques so valuable. For example, the next best offer is a marketing technique to inform customers of a service that is relevant to their interests or purchasing history. Taking this further, when a customer contacts a call center, a predictive model could recommend the next best offer so that the agent can communicate it to the customer while they are still on the phone. Similarly, predictive analytics can be applied to the supply chain to enhance inventory-demand modeling to increase the accuracy of when and where products are shipped to stores, thus decreasing over/under stock issues.

- **Data Visualization:** In the modern digital age, businesses and their employees have used spreadsheet reporting tools to summarize and communicate information. While informative, this technique is static, and in the era of advanced analytics, the amount of data and the complexity of analysis are growing exponentially. This has created a need for new ways of displaying and interacting with data. By employing data visualization technologies, users can interact with real-time data in ways that the traditional methods cannot. For example, data visualization tools allow users to plot data on maps. By using different colors and shades, data can be represented in ways that transcend simple charts and graphs. Visualization allows users who consume the data to highlight different sections and see the underlying data pop up. Also, these users can change the display parameters on the fly, enhancing their engagement with the data. We are finding that effective and engaging displays of data open up the analytics-based decision-making process to a broader and more diverse audience.

It is clear that big data, predictive analytics, and visualization are complementary to one other. One cannot adopt one without adopting the others (at least in the long term). All three dimensions help address the explosion of data and the need for timely and actionable analysis. These responses will also bring organizational changes. Typically data analysts have been relegated to the back office, out-of-sight and crunching numbers all day. However, this is changing. Companies will need to create cross-disciplinary teams—combining mathematicians, statisticians, project managers, domain experts, and technologists—to work collaboratively. In other words, it will take a village to effectively integrate analytics throughout an organization.

So it's coming soon to a world near you: information overload, tamed and ready to help you.

Chapter 7

Open the Aperture

Widen Your Lens, But Do So with Discernment

A point of view can be a dangerous luxury when substituted for insight and understanding.

—Marshall McLuhan

It is better to be approximately right than precisely wrong.

—Lord Keynes

No one can possibly achieve any real or lasting success or "get rich" in business by being a conformist.

—J. Paul Getty

This vintage Camel cigarettes ad from 1946 pretty much tells you all you need to know about the problems of relying on expert opinion. There are better ways.
SOURCE: From the collection of Stanford University (http://tobacco.stanford.edu).

I remember striding up to a podium at the Ritz-Carlton in Palm Beach in 1998, taking a deep breath, and then introducing the future President of Mexico. I think most of the audience thought I was kidding. The unknown man who started to speak in heavily accented, but fluent, English was a tall, cowboy-boot-wearing former CEO of Coca-Cola Mexico, who had been elected governor of a pretty obscure state (Guanajuato). He was smiling ear to ear after my introduction, and said that if he ever did become president, all present would be invited to Los Pinos—the Mexican White House. And so it happened. Several years later he was elected, and—as promised—a group of clients and friends of the firm and I were hosted to a private breakfast with now-President Vicente Fox and his cabinet at the splendid Los Pinos presidential compound in Mexico City. One of our CEO attendees, Kevin Roberts, the inspirational and longstanding leader of advertising powerhouse Saatchi & Saatchi, joked with me that he actually had to buy a tie and dress shirt for the occasion—as he ordinarily wore black T-shirts and claimed he no longer even owned a tie. (Ever the outlier, at the time Kevin had arguably the longest commute in the world, being based in New York but living with his family in Auckland, New Zealand.)

What does this story prove? Well, for starters, many regard Vincente Fox's presidency as disappointing, though his dismantling of Mexico's one-party system was, in fairness, a considerable achievement. Actually, the moral of the story is that you and I need to keep seeking out the unconventional, the maverick, and the undiscovered, or else we'll be breathing our own exhaust. I'm constantly talent scouting, and it was a colleague in Latin America who tipped me off to the rising star of Vicente Fox in Mexican political circles long before anyone gave him

You won't learn any-thing new (and useful) by going to the same places and talking to the same people again and again.

much notice. In 2001, I was introduced to a fascinating but unknown MIT-trained engineer named Colin Angle, and I brought him to Rio de Janeiro to be introduced to my clients and to give a talk about the future of robotics for the home. Today Colin is the celebrated founder and CEO of iRobot, maker of the popular Roomba vacuum cleaning robot as well as the PackBot for military use. In short, you won't learn anything new (and useful) by going to the same places and talking to the same people again and again.

Maybe you need to stop by the Coupa Café in Palo Alto to experience the latest venture capital vibe, or perhaps you should try to get yourself invited to Davos—the greatest confab ever built. Times have changed, as the original Davos Symposium of the 1970s (of which A.T. Kearney was an early sponsor) lasted about two weeks so as to give (mostly) European leaders in business and politics plenty of time to talk, listen, ski, and break bread together. The sessions were well attended, the dress was winter-resort casual, and the media (and side events) were not especially in evidence. It was a turbulent time, and early Davos participants were eager to learn, to forge new relationships, and to test new ideas. Needless to say, some things are now different, and it no longer lasts two weeks!

If you're a Davos regular, it might be worth adding the experience of another kind of forum like TED, the roving ideas-worth-sharing conference in which each presenter is given precisely 18 (or five) minutes to speak and make his or her case. I think TED bubbles up with fascinating emerging ideas and people, but not everyone is convinced: Nassim Taleb, of black-swan fame, ever the contrarian, thinks it's a "monstrosity that turns scientists and thinkers into low-level entertainers, like circus performers."

Other examples include PopTech, a gathering for an eclectic mix of businesspeople and creatives, or even Burning Man, the alternative of all alternative meetings that takes place in the Nevada desert each year and is a showcase of spontaneous creativity and innovation. Burning Man, of course, has a few rules, one of which is clothing is optional. The demand for tickets from veteran and would-be "Burners" alike is so intense that the organizers have had to institute a lottery system, and tickets are being scalped for more than 10 times their face value. But once you're there, money won't get you very far, as the only things you can buy are coffee and ice—literally. (It's been widely reported that Google founders Larry Page and Sergey Brin chose Eric Schmidt to be Google's CEO in part because he was the only one of the finalist candidates who'd been to Burning Man.) While of course you need to be wary of the fashionable gurus, self-proclaimed thought leaders, and faddish charlatans of every era, staying put in your home and office and in your comfort zone is actually the riskier path.

As Kevin Roberts puts it, "Being on the road constantly keeps me close to the dynamics that change almost daily . . . Talking and listening to the younger part of the company keeps me brutally in touch."

Vary Your Information Diet

If you only read highbrow publications like *The Economist*, I recommend that you consider regularly browsing the likes of *People, Hello!* and *USA Today*, if only just to expose yourself to completely different interests and points of view. Likewise, if you are immersed in pop culture, sports, and social media, I'd seriously advise you to vary your information intake. Unlike some, I think going on a media diet or fast is neither realistic nor productive: In today's complex world, one needs to be an information omnivore, and ideally a discerning omnivore.

Thinking back to the 1990s, I remember meeting many executives who thought exactly the opposite of what I was advising: that you should literally tune out everything you can't control (consider it background noise), and focus entirely on the few things you can

Unlike some, I think going on a media diet or fast is neither realistic nor productive: In today's complex world, one needs to be an information omnivore, and ideally a discerning omnivore.

control. Of course by the time 9/11 hit, that way of dealing with—or rather not dealing with—our ever more complex world went out the window. Still there were those, like myself, who had preached for years on the importance of peripheral version and on the value of monitoring the external business environment. *Fortune* magazine wrote in the 1990s about the "reflection imperative," "the need to intensify your intelligence gathering—internally and externally," and cited the example of then IBM CEO Lou Gerstner: "Every six weeks he takes his top 40 managers off-site for a two-day retreat . . . dedicated to management learning in nontraditional areas. Each session features an outside speaker who addresses a topic that is peripheral to the immediate concerns of IBM's leadership. These speakers may be academics, executives from other industries, or even representatives of the art world." At the time, many business leaders considered this notion bizarre, a waste of time, or, at best, a form of diversion or corporate entertainment. Few think that way now, though. Again, it's not always obvious where to look for those critical trend signals that you are probably missing.

Jürgen Hambrecht, the recently retired chairman of German chemicals giant BASF, made a practice of bringing in experts from a variety of different fields outside of BASF's core business areas to gain their insights. His reasoning was clear: For BASF to operate with the necessary foresight and peripheral vision that a global company in a competitive environment requires, it needed access to the best minds in the world—and not just in the fields that it knew well. The benefits of Hambrecht's visionary leadership are clearly reflected in BASF's financial performance, which has returned an annual average of 14.1 percent over the past 10 years—not bad considering that this period encompasses the greatest economic dislocation of any of our lives. And his able successor Dr. Kurt Bock has continued in Hambrecht's forward-thinking footsteps.

Here's another suggestion: If you want to tune in to some really interesting trend waves, you should probably regularly check out the likes of *Monocle*, the lavish, inch-thick "briefing on global affairs, business, culture and design" published monthly from London. Yes, it's more than a bit over the top (including the nine kinds of paper stock used to print it), but it is also one useful indicator of emerging trends, some unexpected and even contrarian, despite the rarefied high-fashion aspect. *Monocle* is the brainchild of style guru, media entrepreneur, and information omnivore Tyler Brûlé, who previously founded and sold *Wallpaper** magazine, which was a runaway success in the late 1990s. Dubbed "Mr. Zeitgeist" by the *New York Times*, Brûlé also writes the popular weekly Fast Lane column in London's *Financial Times*. Not everyone's a fan, to be sure, and some have even wondered whether his name is made up (actually it's real: He grew up in Canada to a Canadian father and an Estonian mother). The point isn't that this eclectic and expensive magazine should be your main source of new trend information. It's just that you need to scan constantly for new ideas and new source material, of which this could be one of many fresh sources if you don't already know it.

By the way, another *Financial Times* columnist worth watching for his style tips (and more) is Hong Kong-born entrepreneur and restaurateur Sir David Tang. His grandfather founded the Kowloon Bus Company, and the family was able to send him to school in England as a teenager (even though it's said he spoke little English until he got there). Having sold the Shanghai Tang fashion chain he founded to Swiss-based luxury goods giant Richemont, Sir David managed to become the exclusive distributor for all Cuban cigars sold in the Asia/Pacific region. Now that's a lot of stogies. Although I can't personally endorse this view, there are some who feel that a good cigar or pipe is a perfect way to address every kind of overload (but for the obvious adverse health consequences). As one sage put it, "A pipe is the foundation of contemplation . . . the companion of the wise; and the man who smokes, thinks like a philosopher and acts like a Samaritan." If that's a bit much, you might also note that the organizers of International Pipe Smokers Day say that "Today's hectic environment almost dictates that we run on full efficiency . . . in a world set at high speed . . . [it's time] to step back [and light up in a spirit] of friend-ship, benevolence, and tranquility." Now put that in your pipe and smoke it. . . .

Clay Johnson, a successful practitioner of the art of insurgent political campaigning using the Internet, makes the point that it's not so much information overload people are dealing with, but rather information overconsumption of the wrong kind. Taking a page from the nutritionists, he thinks we read and watch too much over-processed information—the data equivalent of bleached flour and refined sugar—from recycled sources that merely affirm what we already think.

Add to that the fact that media of all kinds are under severe profit pressures and you also have the phenomenon of churnalism: press releases that get turned into content more or less word for word by editors who have little time or budget to do independent reporting or thinking. In fact, a study conducted by Cardiff University found that 80 percent of stories in Britain's main newspapers were not original content, and that just 12 percent of news stories were generated by reporters. The results at times can be humorous—in 2009 a filmmaker named Chris Atkins posted a sham press release about a fictitious product called a penazzle (supposedly a tattoo for the male—ahem—nether regions). Newspapers began reporting on this novel innovation the next day—with large parts of the press release simply copied and pasted. But the sepa-ration of thought and review from journalism can have more pernicious consequences, particularly when it brings about a reduction in the quality of public debate. And now in the United

> *. . . it's not so much information overload people are dealing with, but rather information overconsumption of the wrong kind. . . . we read and watch too much over-processed information—the data equivalent of bleached flour and refined sugar—from recycled sources that merely affirm what we already think.*

States we also see the rise of politically partisan mainstream media like Fox News on the right and MSNBC on the liberal side—a phenomenon not seen in the United States since the 1800s—further polarizing, confusing, and confounding public understanding and alignment on critical questions of the day.

Be Wary of Conventional Wisdom and the Usual Experts

Every organization needs to have a vision of the future. Strategy and action are impossible without it. The problem, however, is fundamental: The time arrow moves only in one direction, to paraphrase William Janeway, sometime vice-chairman of private equity firm Warburg Pincus. The future doesn't exist yet, and we are invincibly ignorant of what is ahead. So we typically do things that are actually counterproductive: We grasp for forecasts or expert predictions that extrapolate trends based on where things are today, or worse, we stay glued to the rear-view mirror. These tacks generally impede, rather than enhance, our ability to see beyond the horizon. We hold on to seeming certainties or widely accepted truisms: for example, that real estate always goes up; that the (now former) Mubarek regime is stable; that the age of the business cycle is over; that Putin, despite his recent win, will remain unchallenged in Russia for years and decades to come as he seeks additional presidential terms; that the planet is cooling and approaching a new Ice Age (as we thought in the 1970s). . . .

Forecasts based on current trends are potentially dangerous, as they create a false sense of insight and reassurance. Conventional use of expert opinion is—perhaps surprisingly—just as bad. For example, the University of California, Berkeley's landmark study of expert predictions looked at 82,000 predictions over 25 years by 300 leading economists. It turned out that expert views were no better than random guesses, and, worse, the more famous or eminent the expert, the less accurate the prediction!

. . . the University of California, Berkeley's landmark study of expert predictions looked at 82,000 predictions over 25 years by 300 leading economists. It turned out that expert views were no better than random guesses, and, worse, the more famous or eminent the expert, the less accurate the prediction!

Beyond mere fame or eminence, even those with the spark of real genius don't always get it right. Tom Watson, Senior, the pioneering head of IBM from 1914 to 1956, is supposed to have said in the 1940s, "I think there is a world market for maybe five computers." In the late Victorian era, the brilliant British scientist Lord Kelvin went on record with such views as, "Radio has no future," "Heavier-than-air flying machines are impossible," and "X-Rays will prove to be a hoax." Entire books are filled with such now-amusing bloopers spoken by the great and the good in past epochs. I wouldn't want to be too hard on these late gentlemen, for some of our predictions will look equally absurd to future generations. That's not my point.

The point is this: There are a number of separate problems that make forecasting with the help of brand-name experts seriously problematic, even dangerous—and almost always a snapshot of lagging, rather than leading, indicators. The first is the omnipresent temptation to fight the last war that we all have, and subject-matter experts are no different from you or me on this score. Forecasters typically expect the future to be like the present, only 15 percent more so. Sort of like saying the weather tomorrow will be a bit like today. However, some forecasters want to make a bolder prediction that hits you between the eyes, and so they overestimate the effects of some new driving forces (technology or whatever) over the short run, while possibly underestimating them in the long run. To quote the title from an intriguing book: *Where's My Jetpack?* Finally, we still have a lot to learn from the still-young fields of behavioral economics and neuroscience, which are helping us understand our most deeply ingrained cognitive biases, so that we can be conscious of them and correct for them when possible.

I find that, of the major drivers of global change (more on these later), two forces that are consistently misinterpreted are the impacts of technological and demographic change. The first invites the very uneven over- and underestimations that I just described, whereas the latter is nearly always demonstrated as being a smooth, straight line. While the reaction is opposite, the cause for error in both cases is the same—following the immediate trend without fundamental questions about what could change.

Take technology. I referenced earlier a current school of thought that contends that modern technology outside the IT space has plateaued. The data driving this assertion comes from the observation that the digital revolution had its boom, then its bust, and, while somewhat recovered, is currently in a growth flatline. But Brian Arthur argues that most technology revolutions take decades to fully take hold, and that viewed in this context the digital revolution is very much in its early stages. Referencing Schumpeter, Arthur also argues that "technology arrives in clusters—with electrification come dynamos, generators, transformers, switch gear, power distribution systems; with mass production and the automobile come production lines, modern assembly methods, 'scientific management,' road systems, oil refineries, traffic control. These clusters, if they are important, define an era. They eventually change the way business is done, even the way society is conducted." This is what today's doubters will miss by having an insufficiently long historical lens through which to view current trends.

With demographics, the data is much more reliable (we know, for example, with relative certainty, how many 25-year-olds will be alive in 25 years, because it's very closely correlated with the number of births this year), but the interpretation of that data is where too many forecasters miss the mark. Quite simply, the assumption is typically that a particular demographic group in the future will exhibit characteristics, needs, and behaviors very similar to that group today, and conclusions are drawn from that basis. Much of the developed world is facing a tremendous fiscal challenge as a result of this failed assumption—when the modern welfare state was created with retirement ages at 65 or higher (German Chancellor Otto von Bismarck, commonly credited with introducing the first state-funded pension system in the 1880s, actually set the retirement age somewhat higher at 70), it was assumed that into the future most 65-year-olds would behave similarly by dying. When this turned out not to be the case, and modern medicine has added decades to life expectancy, we have an age-overhang in national budgets. Of course, most analysts projecting future budget deficits are also assuming that into the future most 65-year-olds will behave similarly by retiring, and we will see if this is in fact the case (a recent Associated Press poll for example, showed that 73 percent of American Baby Boomers were planning to work well past retirement age).

Interestingly, there is often very public acceptance of the notion that straight-line forecasting can be highly misleading (sometimes laughably so), but at the same time there can be too little will to adopt an alternative. Table 7.1 was produced by the Congressional Research Service, the respected nonpartisan research arm of the U.S. Congress, in a 2009 report examining past predictions of Medicare (the U.S. entitlements program that provides healthcare for elderly and disabled Americans) insolvency. The report shows that nearly from the date of Medicare's inception in 1965, the program was deemed to go bankrupt in a very short time. Forty-five years later it still has not (yet is, of course, projected to do so in relatively short order).

What changed to repeatedly stave off Medicare's fiscal disaster were a number of small adjustments that static forecasts could not capture. Why, then, does the U.S. government continue to publish, year after year, a report that is so demonstrably inaccurate as to be useless, rather than replacing it with something more analytically meaningful? Perhaps because both civil service and political leaders would have to show a difficult-to-find combination of courageous and properly incentivized leadership to change an entrenched process.

Combining the mistakes of misjudging trends in both technology and demographics can lead to some spectacularly wrong forecasts, as Thomas Malthus demonstrated in his treatise *An Essay on the Principle of Population*, published in six editions between 1798 and 1826. He predicted that growing populations among the working class would lead to famine (it didn't). Paul Erlich made the same mistake in his

Table 7.1: Year of Projected Insolvency of the Hospital Insurance Trust Fund in Past Trustees' Reports

Year of Trustees' Report	Year of Insolvency
1970	1972
1971	1973
1972	1976
1973	none indicated
1974	none indicated
1975	late 1990s
1976	early 1990s
1977	late 1980s
1978	1990
1979	1992
1980	1994
1981	1991
1982	1987
1983	1990
1984	1991
1985	1998
1986	1996
1987	2002
1988	2005
1989	—[a]
1990	2003
1991	2005
1992	2002
1993	1999
1994	2001
1995	2002
1996	2001
1997	2001
1998	2008
1999	2015
2000	2025
2001	2029
2002	2030
2003	2026
2004	2019
2005	2020
2006	2018
2007	2019
2008	2019
2009	2017

[a] Contained no long-range projections.

SOURCE: Intermedia projections of various H1 trustees's reports, 1970 to 2009.

1968 book *The Population Bomb*, a doomsday scenario undone by the widespread adoption of nitrogen fertilizer that raised crop yields to feed the world. Almost by definition, these two drivers of technology and population determine levels of growth, income, and prosperity. Economic output, after all, is simply a multiplication of the number of people working (a demographic factor) with their level of productivity (determined in no small part by technology). Underestimating or misinterpreting the implications of these two drivers has correspondingly significant impact on the success of a forecast.

As for expert opinion and prognostications, in an even more dubious category are those experts who have been specifically hired to muddy the waters and create doubt, and the tobacco industry's program of the 1960s and 1970s is only the most obvious example.

As for expert opinion and prognostications, in an even more dubious category are those experts who have been specifically hired to muddy the waters and create doubt, and the tobacco industry's program of the 1960s and 1970s is only the most obvious example. You have to give them some credit for their audacity: The "independent" organization Associates for Research in the Science of Enjoyment (great acronym: ARISE) was among several set up with industry support, in this case to seek evidence for the hypothesis that cigarette smoking actually boosts the immune system through pleasure and relaxation. Buddy, can you spare a light?

Questioning the opinions of experts is not the same thing as going sailing without a map or compass. Humor aside, experts are called that for a reason: They are typically people who have devoted a lifetime of study to a particular field. I'm not saying that you shouldn't listen to experts, but only that you do so under three conditions.

- Approach expert opinion with a reasoned, respectful skepticism. Always look for their underlying assumptions and biases before accepting their views.

- Be flexible in your acceptance. Always be prepared to change both your view and your plans when warranted (remember the quote earlier from Lord Keynes). Peter Drucker always emphasized that strategy is a sense of direction around which you improvise—you must have a clear vision of where you are heading, but still be able to nimbly tack with the wind to get there.
- Be certain that the scope of the expert (and non-expert) opinion you solicit is sufficiently broad-based—and be omnivorous.

The Problem of Being Right Too Early

Sometimes a really outstanding thinker is right too early, as legendary bond manager and PIMCO co-founder Bill Gross probably was in 2011 when he got out of U.S. Treasuries (just before they rallied massively yet again). But he may well be correct that U.S. paper is the last thing you want to be holding for the long haul. Frankly, I'd rather be right too early than too late, given a choice.

But how do you distinguish the truly farsighted expert from the mostly mediocre rest? How do you separate out the trend from the trendy? I realize some executives and politicians are so desperate for foresight that they literally consult soothsayers. Maybe you've heard of French clairvoyant Yaguel Didier, who has a six-month client waiting list? (She says, "Seeing the future is tiring work.") I'm afraid there is no Geiger counter available, but here are some clues and suggestions. For starters, the most remarkable people of all combine depth with breadth, and cultivate a wide knowledge and an even wider intake. My alma mater, the University of Chicago, is only just over a century old, having been founded in one go by John D. Rockefeller, and it claims —I think accurately—to have generated the largest total number of Nobel prizes in history. Why would this be so? Well, some commentators say that the University of Chicago—set off the beaten path in a society dominated by bicoastal elites—made room for brainy oddballs and iconoclasts. The "Chicago boys" trained by Milton Friedman and his circle famously made free-market economics respectable again after the post-World World II flirtation with state socialism in most parts of the world, but the Chicago influence goes well beyond economics to almost every field and discipline under the sun.

Do you know the old saying, "It doesn't take a genius"? Well, sometimes and for some problems, it does take a genius. You probably know that there are agencies that represent professional athletes, authors, and actors. A few years ago we saw the establishment of Geniisis, the world's first agents for geniuses. The firm is the brainchild of California technology executive and longtime Oriel College, Oxford board member Patrick Riley. What's interesting here is that you don't ask Riley to hire a genius or assemble a team of geniuses for general chitchat. This is all about finding the right brainpower to try to solve a specific wicked (typically business) problem that has eluded every solution—for example, the looming shortage of certain scarce elements in the periodic table that have been essential to the latest generation of consumer electronics. This is no academic exercise.

Pierre Wack, a Shell executive I will mention more in the final chapter, was the modern father of scenario planning, but he cultivated wide interests (even in religious mysticism). Royal Dutch Shell was, in the 1950s and 1960s, the weakest of the Seven Sisters (as the seven largest oil companies were then called). *Forbes* magazine called it the ugly sister, lacking the vast reserves and key Arab world relationships that the other leading petroleum giants enjoyed. So Shell had to think differently. More so than their peer group companies, Shell encouraged executives to ". . . cultivate orchids and lead chamber orchestras. . . . One managing director, during the years of his tenure, published well-received histories of Nigeria and Turkey." The whole fascinating story is well beyond the scope of this book, but Shell's revolution in creative thinking and applied foresight actually allowed it to get a tangible leg up. By the time the energy crisis and shocks rolled around in the early 1970s, it was better prepared than its competitors mentally and operationally. By the late 1970s, Shell was no longer the ugly sister, but had catapulted itself to the top during an era of disruption and discontinuity.

Marshall McLuhan, the late Canadian futurist, is best known for such memorable expressions as "the global village" and "the medium is the message." But who remembers that a key aspect to his uncanny foresight was a deliberate study of many disciplines, and also of the spaces between disciplines? Born on the Alberta prairie, McLuhan studied literature, philosophy, and theology in Canada and later at Cambridge University in England, before immersing himself in an uncommonly broad study of culture and technology. During the 1960s and 1970s, he became one of the world's most famous people (and a national icon in Canada), but remained a self-disciplined, buttoned-down seer in still prim-and-proper Toronto during an otherwise chaotic, psychedelic era. (Counterculture guru Timothy Leary is said to have picked some of his best lines from McLuhan.) In 1962, McLuhan predicted, "A computer as a research and communication instrument could enhance retrieval, obsolesce mass library organization, retrieve the individual's encyclopedic function, and flip into a private line to speedily tailored data of a saleable kind."

Now that's what I call foresight.

Tap into Remarkable People and Places

If you want to expose yourself to remarkable people who are emerging, and if you want to tap into the world's key brainpower hubs, you also have to realize that reputations are lagging indicators. One of the reasons for this is that once a person is established they have too much to lose by saying something counter-intuitive—or adventurous. On the other hand, those trying to make a name have an incentive to say something crazy and hope that it sticks. The trick is to be omnivorous and discerning enough to be able to separate the has-beens and the hacks from the genuinely insightful. As for the durability of reputations, the new dean of Harvard Business School, Indian-born Nitin Nohria, has shaken up a tried-but-true MBA curriculum that many felt was resting on its laurels for too long. In doing so, he invited friends and faculty of HBS to think about what the world's top 10 universities are today and what they were a century ago. Here is my attempt to reproduce the two notional lists, based in part on the Shanghai Jiao Tong rankings and other sources:

The World's Top 10 Universities—2012 (alphabetical order)

California Institute of Technology
University of California (System)
University of Cambridge
University of Chicago
Harvard University
Massachusetts Institute of Technology
University of Oxford
Princeton University
Stanford University
Yale University

The World's Top 10 Universities—1912 (alphabetical order)

University of Berlin
University of Bonn
University of Breslau
University of Cambridge
University of Göttingen
University of Halle
University of Heidelberg
University of Jena
University of Leipzig
University of Oxford

Notice any differences? Oxford and Cambridge are there on both notional lists, but all the others have changed. In 1912, arguably eight of the 10 best universities were German, and today eight of the 10 are American. What happened to the German schools? A hundred years ago, Germany was pumping out Nobel prizes in the sciences like no tomorrow; German research universities were the envy of the world; and German companies, such as BASF in chemicals, were world leaders. Today, while BASF is still a world leader, the other things are no longer true. (In fact, Jürgen Hambrecht, the visionary former head of BASF that I mentioned earlier, is currently working very hard to do something positive for his country's educational outlook, but that's another story.) Nazi anti-Semitism and political correctness proved highly damaging to German academe—the very opposite of openness to diversity and inclusion, to say the least. The later postwar expansion in student numbers, without a corresponding increase in university resources, finished the job at once-vaunted places like Bonn and Heidelberg. In the meantime, the initiative had already passed to the great American research universities.

Likewise, even Harvard can't afford to be complacent. New brainpower hubs are bubbling up in unexpected places, and you should see them for yourself before your competition does. I remember hearing John Gage, then chief scientist of Sun Microsystems, tell a group of CEOs that looking at college and university rankings was like looking at the stars in the nighttime sky—you see the light, but actually you're looking into the past. If you're looking for new light, he said you should see who's winning the world computer programming championships now, for example. Ever heard of the ACM-ICPC International Collegiate Programming Contest sponsored by IBM? Well, the recent results may surprise you. There is some drop-dead unbelievable applied brainpower coming out of some (to us) obscure Chinese institutions and also out of a veritable Slavic brotherhood of universities and technical institutes in Poland, Russia, Ukraine, and even Belarus. Canada gets an honourable (er, honorable) mention with its MIT-like University of Waterloo. But have you heard of Perm State (not Penn State, but Perm State University in Russia), or how about Zhejiang University?

Other examples? Israel, once famous for its socialist-style kibbutz collective

> *New brainpower hubs are bubbling up in unexpected places, and you should see them for yourself before your competition does. I remember hearing John Gage, then chief scientist of Sun Microsystems, tell a group of CEOs that looking at college and university rankings was like looking at the stars in the nighttime sky—you see the light, but actually you're looking into the past.*

farms, is now buzzing with scientists, entrepreneurs, and new companies; the Technion campus in Haifa is a new MIT in every sense. There's a reason why Israel is now called the "Start-up Nation" (also the title of a recent book about the Israel effect in the technological realm). Since 2005, Israel has seen GDP grow by more than 34 percent, compared with a relatively meager 6.4 percent in the United States. Israel now has more companies traded on the NASDAQ than Korea, Japan, Singapore, China, India, and Europe combined.

Take Poland. After the fall of the Berlin Wall, it seemed less exciting than its Central European neighbors like the Czech Republic and Hungary because it was considered too big and too poor to get anywhere fast. Now that size, location, and heft (40 million people) has turned into a distinct advantage, allowing the Poles to take back their historic place among Europe's six largest nations (the others being Great Britain, Germany, France, Italy, and Spain). During the recent period of heart-stopping crises and downturn in Europe, Poland was the only EU country to avoid recession and keep growing robustly. In fact, the country is enjoying its best period of economic growth, political stability, and cultural and technological creativity in about 300 years. While Poland's discovery of large-scale shale gas reserves has gotten lots of press, a less well-known development is the vibrancy of the Aviation Valley in and around Rzeszów, which has been a pioneering aerospace hub since the 1930s.

Poland also has an interesting, youngish power couple to go with its raised game and bigger ambitions: witty, Oxford-educated Foreign Minister (and sometime presidential candidate) Radek Sikorski and his American wife, Anne Applebaum, a Pulitzer Prize-winning author and journalist. (The fact that Anne is a Jewish-American also says something about Poland today.) Poles quip that in the last 30 years they've gone from being in Soviet-controlled Eastern Europe to being back in Central Europe and now to being seen as part of hard-working, fiscally responsible Northern Europe, without ever moving.

And if the BRICs are old hat, what about the CRAB countries (Canada, Russia, Australia, Brazil)? This acronym—coined by star investment manager Renee Haugerud (who started her career as a grain trader at privately-held agribusiness giant Cargill)—hasn't really stuck, but the idea behind it is interesting. In the case of the first three—Canada, Russia, and Australia—you have countries with relatively small populations (compared with their surface area), benefiting from climate change in the Arctic in the case of the first two and holding a large slice of the world's natural resources and fresh water between them (the exception on water is bone-dry Australia). The fourth has developed an amazing level of agricultural productivity and commercial creativity. Brazil is perhaps the most unusual case of all, given the country's long history of disappointing investors and friends: The Brazilian business school called the Fundação Getúlio Vargas may not be on your radar screen yet, but it should be.

And a growing number of Brazilian enterprises are truly world-class competitors, from Embraer and Bank Itaú, to Braskem and AmBev. The world's largest brewer, AB InBev, which bought American icon Anheuser-Busch, is run from Europe by a dynamic management team that has deep Brazilian roots. David Neeleman, the Brazilian-born American (and Mormon) founder of discount airline JetBlue, is back in Brazil again, now running his fast-growing airline Azul (Portuguese for *blue*). Brazilian powerhouse Vale is one of the world's two largest metals and mining companies, and it has opened up massive, new distribution facilities around the world—from the Port of Sohar in Oman to Subic Bay in the Philippines (formerly a home of the U.S. Navy). One can almost hear echoes of the great trading companies of an earlier age, including the British and Dutch East India companies.

As Canadian thinker Marshall McLuhan emphatically noted, a point of view is no substitute for real insight into what's going on. So get on a plane to São Paulo—and to other places you need to experience for yourself. Do something different. Widen your lens. Take it all in, as the discerning omnivore you are (or ought to be).

Chapter 8

Turning Pixels into a Clearer Picture

Applying Scenario Thinking to Make a Better Future Possible

Scenario planning is ... aimed at ... foresight in contexts of accelerated change, greater complexity and genuine uncertainty.
—Pierre Wack, pioneer of scenario thinking and late Head of Group Planning, Royal Dutch Shell

Don't count out the West—the civilization that brought you Rembrandt and the non-stick frying pan.
—Josef Joffe, Editor and Publisher of *Die Zeit*, Hamburg, and Fellow, Hoover Institution, Stanford University

There is only one past and one present, but there are multiple possible futures. And there is an art (and science) to learning how to think about, enable, and act on the future we envision.
SOURCE: Age fotostock/SuperStock.

"**M**eet me at the General Motors Futurama around lunchtime." That's what I told my parents when we went to the 1964–65 New York World's Fair, the last of the great world expos that tried to showcase dreams of progress. I admit it was exciting: From the Bell System's pavilion with its picture phone (which anticipated Skype by about 50 years) to more mundane innovations, such as the electric toothbrush, the credit card, and formica laminated plastic, the sense of promise was infectious. General admission was two dollars for adults and one dollar for kids. Walt Disney's magic was behind many of the attractions at the World's Fair, and some of them were later moved lock, stock, and barrel to a 10-year-old Disneyland in Southern California—where Tomorrowland featured monorails and People Movers, and the corporate sponsors included TWA, Monsanto, American Motors, Richfield Oil, Dutch Boy Paint, and GE. Both the Fair and Disneyland showed us the promise—and the limitations—of trying to imagine what the future might hold. In more recent years, the Disney imagineers have displayed a sense of humor about how their 1960s vision of the Space Age had become embarrassingly dated; so they've played up its retro-futuristic, Jules Verne, steampunk flavor, joking that Tomorrowland is "the future that never was."

That's the problem with futurism: It's frequently so far off-base that it has about as much real-life utility as using last year's pulp science fiction to build your corporate strategy. So what's the alternative? Actually, there are two main methodologies my colleagues and I use with clients around the world, day in and day out: scenario planning and horizon scanning. They are not so much about predicting the future as they are about informing the present, so that organizations can

Actually, there are two main methodologies my colleagues and I use with clients around the world, day in and day out: scenario planning and horizon scanning. They are not so much about predicting the future as they are about informing the present so that organizations can develop alternative scenarios of the future they can act upon now.

develop alternative scenarios of the future they can act upon now. It's important to note that these are real disciplines, with bodies of knowledge that even relatively passive users need to understand—so do-it-yourself scenario planning makes about as much sense as DIY eye surgery. (Friends don't let friends become amateur futurists.) So do yourself and your organization a favor, and get some basic training at the very least. Various universities and stand-alone institutes offer crash courses, but the best of the bunch is probably Oxford University's scenarios program. While Oxford was very late to the business school game, it has carved out a special niche in the foresight area, with a regular scenarios program done in collaboration with my firm for clients as well as open-enrollment programs. (They even give graduates of their flagship five-day scenarios executive program Oxford alumni status.) I might add that the full foresight toolkit goes well beyond scenario planning and horizon scanning and includes such related disciplines as modeling/simulations (wargaming), backcasting, and real-money prediction markets.

Scenario planning was originally pioneered by Royal Dutch Shell, the RAND Corporation, the Hudson Institute, and the Stanford Research Institute, later renamed SRI International (where I spent a decade). The discipline is universally known as scenario planning, though I think a better description is scenario-based strategic planning, and there are several rigorous methods—inductive, deductive, probabilistic, intuitive logics, causal layered—to use some of the clunky official nomenclature. It's worth noting that the word scenario gets used pretty casually (and even sloppily) these days, and the word can mean many things to many people. The annual, star-studded Cannes

Film Festival even gives a top prize each year to the best scenarist—which, though it can mean a writer of either scenarios or screenplays, is usually translated into English as *screenwriter*.

Scenario planning, in many ways, has been a central focus of my career, starting out as I did in the energy industry, where the discipline is widely accepted, and spending time at SRI, which had been at the forefront of methodological research on scenario planning. I mentioned my 2005 book, *World Out of Balance*, in the context of having successfully predicted a period of global economic instability when this seemed like a highly unlikely prospect at the time. In fact, *World Out of Balance* was written to make the case for scenario planning as a discipline, and to outline the methodology and approach that we developed at A.T. Kearney. Using this methodology, viewing the world through the lens of fundamental drivers rather than popular trends (more on this further on) and casting out conventional, linear forecasts in favor of less rigid and constrained possibilities of the future was how we were able to make a forecast that seems remarkably prescient seven years later. Prescient, perhaps, but truly based on what my friend John Gray, then of the London School of Economics, called "powerfully imagined and rigorously researched" scenarios that serve as tools for understanding the future.

At its simplest, scenario planning is a way of developing plausible stories about what the future might look like without being constrained by the limitations of today's generally accepted assumptions. At A.T. Kearney, in any given case, we model multiple scenarios of the future using what we regard as the five fundamental drivers of change:

- Globalization.
- Demographics.
- Consumption patterns.
- Natural resources and the environment.
- Regulation and activism, with technology as an additional meta-driver underpinning the others, and wildcards representing other low-probability, high-impact events.

The process itself stimulates new ideas and nimbleness of mind and receptivity to action, as well as creating possibilities of the future that can be seized. The folks at Oxford like to call this the canary in the mind, with scenario planning playing the role that canaries used to in coal mines: If the canary started behaving strangely (or, worse, dropped dead), it was an important but subtle sign of impending change or danger.

Scenario planning yields a number of benefits—it can be used to set strategy in a more thorough and flexible way than traditional forecasting, serve as an early warning system for changes around the bend, and uncover blind spots and biases in thinking. An often overlooked aspect, however, is the role that scenarios can play as communications tools to build internal and external alignment. A management team that has gone through a flexible visioning exercise together is collectively more aware of and alert to the needs and market realities faced by customers, and is more aligned and focused as a result. Scenarios can also be used as tools to drive shareholder value by communicating the context of strategic decisions externally (as a colleague of mine used to say, "talking with the street").

It's important to note that scenario planning is a process more than a product. It is an iterative development of alternative future visions best done in close collaboration with the leaders and decision-makers who will be using the scenarios as the basis for current and future action. If the scenarios are created in a vacuum and simply handed down to an organization, it's difficult to generate the buy-in or enthusiasm necessary to truly influence decision-making (*buy-in*, of course, is one of the more maligned management consulting buzzwords—in the context of scenario planning a simpler word might actually be *belief*). Our friends at Oxford refer to the scenario planning projects they work on as interventions—activities taken to help arrest the current

The folks at Oxford like to call this the canary in the mind, with scenario planning playing the role that canaries used to in coal mines: If the canary started behaving strangely (or, worse, dropped dead), it was an important but subtle sign of impending change or danger.

(usually either erroneous or poorly informed) course of an organization and redirect it by providing leaders with new tools to navigate by.

This discipline is equally applicable to governments, and the Republic of Singapore has probably been the heaviest public policy user of scenario thinking since its independence. Considering that the place around 1960 was a small, poor, dirty city-state with a rotting dockyard, no resources (or air conditioning), and a dangerous insurgency movement, the Singaporeans couldn't afford to be conventional or merely incremental—and they haven't been. For obvious reasons, most of the best scenario work is not in the public domain, but rather under strict lock-and-key: Scenarios developed for strategic use by corporations, governments, and intelligence services are by definition highly confidential.

One of the better known, ironically, of such confidential reports is the quadrennial National Intelligence Estimate, timed to provide each incoming (or returning) U.S. president with a scenario-based outlook of the world for their term. The report, prepared by the National Intelligence Council, is well known because the high-level outtakes are released to the public, while the more in-depth (and classified) explanations and implications are reserved for official consumption.

Scenarios are most useful when they are developed for a specific client or a specific purpose. Still, general, global, macro scenarios can provide some intellectual nourishment and food for thought. Royal Dutch Shell's website displays their public scenarios for the energy environment in 2050, which were unveiled in 2009 and updated in 2011. Sony has published macro scenarios for 2025—FutureScapes— with the scenarios ranging from a happy vision of hyper-innovation to some less happy (even in some cases dystopian, *Blade Runner*-like) alternative futures called shared ownership, centralized survival, and prosperity redefined. (For some of the latter scenarios, having a well-stocked survivalist-style bunker in Montana might not be an entirely bad preparation.) Like the National Intelligence Estimate, the depth and content of the public releases tend to be somewhat different from the private, confidential versions. But this reveals another important use for scenarios as communication tools with external stakeholders.

Another example of scenarios designed to stimulate public discussion are those developed by the Swiss federal government—Perspectives 2025. The Swiss federal chancellery released four possible scenarios for the external environment the country will face in 2025: Global Integration/Regional Integration (globalization and mobility); Global Integration/Regional Fragmentation (the Renaissance of Asia); Global Fragmentation/Regional Fragmentation (return to Swiss traditions); and Global Fragmentation/Regional Integration (Europe as superpower). The symbols of the four scenarios are, not surprisingly, a globe, a Chinese dragon, a Swiss edelweiss, and the logo of the European Union. While we can debate the relative plausibility of these scenarios, it's interesting to see what strategists in Bern are thinking when they look at the world outside the Alps.

As for corporate examples, GE's 2011 Annual Report displays an interesting flash of scenario thinking. The GE folks say they are watching four things:

- China (will it grow?).
- Europe (plan for a recession).
- The United States (could be a pleasant surprise).
- Inflation (the wild card—prepare for high inflation).

Powerfully Imagined and Rigorously Researched: The Structure of Scenario Thinking

The eternal yin and yang of the scenario planning discipline is to create scenarios that stretch the imagination and broaden the thinking of the users (internal or external clients, stakeholders outside the organization, or individuals making decisions), while remaining sufficiently grounded and plausible so as to be usable and actionable. Striking the right balance is key, and it is the difference between a fruitful intervention and a digression into easily dismissed fantasy. It's not often that management consultants are compared to artists, but successful scenario planning is about truly finding the right blend of art and science to construct alternative visions of the future.

First, the art. One of the most difficult elements of a scenario planning exercise, a challenge usually encountered at the very beginning, is to persuade the participants that we are not in the business of predicting or forecasting the future. It's always rewarding when one of the scenarios that you outlined does in fact largely manifest itself in actual events, as was the case with the Castles and Moats scenario I developed for my earlier book *World Out of Balance*, but the goal of prediction cannot be the primary objective of scenario planning. (Although I must note that a colleague recently approached me on a trip to New Delhi, and told me that having recently re-read *World Out of Balance*, he couldn't believe how well we had been able to anticipate the Arab Spring.) But when scenarios are forcibly turned into forecasts, the scenarios become constrained by the inherent biases and leanings that each of the participants inevitably brings with them—closing off possibilities rather than opening them up. In an effort to get the right answer, people typically become unwilling to move outside of their natural comfort zones and truly tackle uncertainty. The past, which of course is where all of the evidence is, becomes the sole foundation for our views on the future. Cognitive biases and decision traps are allowed to take hold and the entire rationale for engaging in scenario planning rather than conventional forecasting is compromised.

It's easy to understand why this is so. Human nature craves certainty, and definitive answers always seem likely to be better received by corporate management and boards of directors than compelling questions. This can be especially difficult in a management-consulting context, where consultants feel obligated to provide their clients with a single, clear answer to a difficult and challenging problem about the future, rather than a series of plausible alternatives. There is clearly a comfort factor to overcome, but the good news is that if the scenario planning process is making you or your client feel uncomfortable, then you're probably doing a good job. Good scenarios capture and embrace uncertainty while challenging conventional wisdom, even in the face of discomfort at the practitioner and client level. As my friend Rafael Ramírez of Oxford University likes to say about his own scenario planning exercises, his thumb and forefinger placed close together: "If you're not this close to being fired, you're not pushing far enough with the scenarios."

What makes the difference between compelling, imaginative scenarios that stretch thinking and shake biases and valuable scenario-based tools for corporate strategy is the rigor, and structure that a scenario planner brings to the project, in addition to prodigious imagination. It is the science that balances the art. Futurist and occasional A.T. Kearney collaborator Ryan Matthews calls scenarios that are packed with imagination but lacking structure "intellectual Chinese food," in reference to the common American misperception that one is left hungry again a couple hours after a meal at a Chinese restaurant (Ryan lives in Michigan, where perhaps a quality Szechuan or Cantonese establishment has yet to open in his neighborhood).

All scenario work begins with an outside-in look at the business environment (I always try not to get overly academic in the way that I approach scenario planning, but Kees van der Heijden, one of the founders of modern scenario thinking, calls this the contextual environment). To make all this meaningful to a client or organization, the scenarios explore the interaction of these external forces with a firm's more immediate business environment (to use van der Heijden's term, the transactional environment). But starting with the whole world as the basis for a scenario planning exercise too often leads to boiling the ocean and getting nowhere, so a good framework for thinking about the world is a must.

Earlier in this chapter I referred to the five-drivers framework that we use at A.T. Kearney, which is one such method for categorizing global trends. The essential thinking here is that by having a system by which to categorize the trends that we continuously scan for, these various data points will be more usable and readily available to leverage in our scenario-building projects. To recap, the five drivers are:

- Globalization, or the increasing interconnectedness of economic systems and cultures characterized by movement of people, goods, capital, ideas, and communications across borders.
- Demographics, in which we look not only at current and projected population growth and longevity data, but also at the ways that societies are changing to manage these changes.

- Consumption patterns, which encompass changes in consumer demand, attitudes, and lifestyles, as well as how companies are meeting these shifts.
- Natural resources and the environment, which looks at the effects of climate change, to be sure, but also at resource use and availability patterns across a range of inputs.
- Regulation and activism, which encompass both the overt actions taken by different types of governments (and, it should be noted, these can be either in the form of specific pieces of legislation or in the administrative space) as well as the social and NGO movements that complement, contest, and drive government activity.

In addition, we consider potential wildcards—high-impact, low-probability events of the sort popularized by Nassim Taleb—and the effects that these could have on the trends captured by the five drivers. Finally, the transformative impact of technology is considered as a crosscutting über-driver that can accelerate or redirect the course of each driver. These five drivers together, with the augmenting influences of wildcards and transformative technology captured as well, form a coherent way of organizing data to construct cogent and compelling narratives of the future.

There are a number of similar systems out there (A.T. Kearney's own Erik Peterson developed something similar called the Seven Revolutions when he was at the prestigious Center for Strategic and International Studies), but to me the five-drivers methodology stands out by organizing around the most fundamental forces in the global business environment. This is a critical distinction with alternative methodologies that focus on derivative rather than fundamental indicators.

Once there is a system in place for understanding and organizing the data that will serve as an input for scenario building, the right methodology can be selected. Here are a couple of notes on scenario-building methodologies

- There is no right choice. There are dozens of competing ways to construct scenarios, but none of them is a silver bullet that solves all futures questions. Rather, the choice depends on the purpose and the circumstances of the scenario intervention. Methodologies differ in their degrees of cost and complexity and in the amount of work they require. Ensuring that the methodology will fit within the time constraints of the intervention, and that the leaders who will ultimately use the scenarios as decision-making tools understand how they were developed, is far more important than one school of futures thought over another.

- The users of the scenarios must be as involved as possible in their creation. Oxford's Rafael Ramírez promotes a one-third, two-thirds rule of thumb to guide scenario planning exercises. One-third of a scenario planner's time should be spent developing the actual scenarios, while two-thirds should be spent involving stakeholders from across the client organization, working through and refining the scenarios with their active participation.

Two of the methodologies that I've found particularly useful in scenario planning engagements (and unlike some of the other, more complex ones, don't require an advanced mathematics or computer science degree) are the inductive and deductive methods (more on these shortly). As I said, one is not better than the other—they are each the right tool for a given situation. The difference between the two lies principally in their appropriateness for a particular intervention, specifically in the amount of time and the level of engagement that can be expected during an intervention. When time is very tight and potential stakeholder engagement is limited, I prefer the deductive method. When time and energy are more readily available, I find that the inductive method can drive toward scenarios with greater depth. A brief explanation of each of these:

In the deductive method of scenario building, the set of available trends (in our case, filtered first by the five-drivers approach) is whittled down to two, around which to base the scenarios. In effect, these two trends are plotted on a two-by-two matrix, and the scenario outcomes are deduced (hence, deductive) from the quadrants of the matrix. That's right, from the whole universe of trends across globalization, demographics, and the rest, two are identified as the primary scenario inputs. How do we determine which are the right trends to build scenarios around? We plot the various trends in order of uncertainty and impact, selecting those with the highest degree of uncertainty and the most significant impact on an organization.

After determining which two trends are both high-impact and highly uncertain, we discuss with the client which two are the most interesting or critical for their organization's future, and use these to create scenarios. The two selected trends are plotted on a two-by-two matrix, and each quadrant in the matrix forms the basis for one scenario narrative. In the illustration below, we chose industry integration and innovation as the two factors around which to base scenarios for the global technology retail industry.

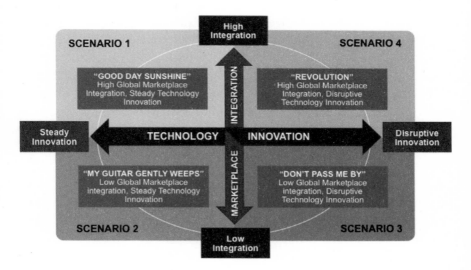

With the deductive method of building scenarios, we plot trends by highest impact and greatest uncertainty, and then take the two most critical or interesting ones to create scenarios in the way shown in this matrix.

Scenarios (in all methodologies) usually have memorable names that participants can use to refer to a specific vision of the future, and this lends scenarios special value as an internal communications tool. It's always interesting (and rewarding) to hear two scenario intervention participants, discussing a point of corporate strategy months after the workshop, say, "Yes, but what happens to that project in a 'Revolution' world?"

The benefit of the deductive method is that the process is fairly straightforward and the scenarios are highly intuitive. Determining the axes can take considerable time to align around, but once formed, the scenario process is easily understood, leading to quicker adoption times. On the other hand, a drawback tends to be that the scenarios themselves are by definition less full bodied than in other approaches.

Rather than focusing on just two trends, the inductive method, by contrast, follows the combined, logical permutations of a larger (potentially infinite) number of trends to form scenarios. Inductive scenario building does not inherently limit the number of trends or data points that are considered, although these are frequently constrained for reasons of practicality. In the inductive process, the potential plausible outcomes of each of the trends is explored and the common interactions between them form the basis for scenarios. Potential plausible outcomes can be a sticking point—the way that a trend's development is described must be based both on solid data (to provide a base case) and on imagination (to provide alternatives). Remember, scenarios are only useful if they are based both in research and in provocative thinking. Throughout the process plausibility and consistency checks must be performed to ensure that trend developments do not contradict one another.

Sound complicated? It is. Project teams can spend weeks (or in some particularly complex exercises, months) working through data and trend analysis. There also needs to be frequent interaction with the client, to ensure that they understand and are aligned with the thinking of the scenario team, and that they have the opportunity to provide their own input as well. But the result of this long process is a set of scenarios that can be remarkably rich in their depth and color. Some of the best-known examples of scenario planning that I referred to earlier in this chapter, such as the National Intelligence Estimate and those from Shell, use the inductive method of scenario building.

Counterfactuals and Other Futures Thinking

Closely related to scenarios, but different, are counterfactuals, which literally mean some alternatives that didn't actually happen, but could have. It's essentially scenario planning in reverse, applying the scenarios to the past rather than the future. Why would this be interesting for us? For starters, we're all already instinctively interested in what-if questions, and most of us have probably been replaying scenarios of all kinds in our minds since we were children. The popular 1931 book, *If It Had Happened Otherwise*, sparked the serious interest in counterfactuals as an actual discipline. It was a set of essays by well-known people of the time speculating how history might have turned out differently had just one

> *Closely related to scenarios, but different, are counterfactuals, which literally mean some alternatives that didn't actually happen, but could have. It's essentially scenario planning in reverse, applying the scenarios to the past rather than the future.*

thing been changed. Winston Churchill, then in the political wilderness (enduring a lull in his career), contributed a speculative piece on how the world would have been different if General Robert E. Lee had won the Battle of Gettysburg, rather than losing it.

You get the picture. What if a starving artist named Adolf Hitler had actually gotten into the Vienna Academy of Fine Arts (where he applied twice, but got rejected)? What if the bullets had missed President Kennedy? What if Mikhail Gorbachev had not come to power in the Soviet Union in the 1980s? What if the Lehman Brothers collapse had been averted by government action? At some point, counterfactuals seem less a method of inquiry and more an amusing parlor game, as critics have called it.

However, there is something useful here for business and policy leaders. There are multiple possible futures, but only one past, which is a real advantage to those of us who are trying to analyze and sift trends and events. Glasgow-born, Oxford-educated, Harvard professor and media commentator Niall Ferguson makes the point that key assumptions about the present and future can be tested "by means of a counterfactual question"—and that "what didn't happen is often as interesting as what did." Ferguson adds, in his book *Virtual History: Alternatives and Counterfactuals*, "Of course we know perfectly well that we cannot travel back in time and do these things differently. But the business of imagining such counterfactuals is a vital part of the way in which we learn. Because decisions about the future are—usually—based on weighing up the potential consequences of the alternative courses of action, it makes sense to compare the actual outcomes of what we did in the past with the conceivable outcomes of what we might [plausibly] have done."

In a similar vein, in 1993, *The Economist* decided to celebrate its 150th anniversary by looking backward and forward—and by asking some 20 luminaries to take a stab at what the next 150 years might have in store for us. The editors naturally hedged their bets by stating, "All forecasts are, in truth, observations about the present and recent past. They are judgments about which trends and which characteristics of today and yesterday are likeliest to endure and to have the most impact on tomorrow."

Some 20 years after that special anniversary issue, how are their prognostications looking? Not bad, actually. Here are some of their predictions (and my editorial comments):

- Politics worldwide will move toward more Swiss-style direct democracy—referendums, popular initiatives, and the like. (They got that right, but, as the California experience shows, is that really a good thing?)
- The United States will become even more politically correct, litigious, and regulation-mad. (Check.)
- Africa's colonial-era borders will be redrawn in favor of both smaller states (e.g., Eritrea) and regional integration. (Let's call that a draw.)
- Race and religion will become more, not less, important in the future. (Got that right.)
- Warfare has a future. (Ditto, unfortunately.)
- Education will be transformed by new technology. (Your call, though it is happening more gradually than we might have expected.)
- Capitalism could sow the seeds of its own demise or at least disasters. (A rather prescient prediction.)

- Televisions and telephones, and the companies that make them, will become obsolete. (That's a hard one to parse given that what we mean by TV or phone has changed radically since 1993.)
- Developments in medicine will range from technologically enabled self-diagnosis to the coming of even more fraught moral and ethical dilemmas. (Bulls-eye.)

While we did not have the 150 years of history that *The Economist* had to look back to, at the time of our management buy-out (MBO), A.T. Kearney was very much both a startup as well as an organization equally inspired and burdened by 86 years of history. Similar to the exercise they went through, we looked back in order to think ahead. Although many of my partners were eager to act first and reflect later, I cautioned them to pause. At our first post-MBO worldwide partners meeting in Cannes in 2006, we adopted the theme "Firm foundation, Forward focus" to represent an expanded vision (and expansion plans) that were simultaneously firmly grounded in our history, values, and cultural DNA.

This kind of anniversary rethink leads us right into my next point: In addition to scenario building, my colleagues and I also employ horizon scanning, which I personally prefer to call over-the-horizon scanning. This is in many ways the very opposite of collecting and aggregating conventional expert views, and trying to find some kind of homogenized expert consensus. We deliberately seek out unconventional views, maverick thinkers, and raw, unfiltered intelligence from unusual sources—some of which may become inputs for the scenario process as well. You need to be an intellectual omnivore with a highly varied, and changing, diet of ideas and information. And as I've already urged, you also need to get on a plane and take your own measure of things on the ground—frequently, and to far-flung places outside your normal comfort zone. The alternative is stale thinking leading either to inaction or yesterday's (ineffective) tactics and platitudes. People and organizations need to think unconventionally in order to act decisively in new ways, addressing new world realities and changing demands. Think again about the decision traps that I've mentioned several times before in this book.

This is in many ways the very opposite of collecting and aggregating conventional expert views, and trying to find some kind of homogenized expert consensus. We deliberately seek out unconventional views, maverick thinkers, and raw, unfiltered intelligence from unusual sources—some of which may become inputs for the scenario process as well.

As for real-money prediction markets, they remain in their infancy but offer some intriguing hints about other useful tools that are emerging for divining the future. The much-ballyhooed Iowa Electronic Markets runs several online futures markets where contract payoffs are based on real-world events like political outcomes; for example, the quadrennial presidential election market where payoffs will be based on the U.S. popular vote in the general election. Past market trading is said to have offered a better picture of the evolving reality (and eventual outcomes) than political polling, and there has been fierce academic debate on whether that's the case and why. I think it probably has something to do with the fact that market participants with real insight and the courage of their convictions (to put money on the table) are trading, rather than random members of the general public. The Iowa Electronic Markets are operated for research and teaching purposes that help them get around U.S. restrictions on online gambling and unregulated futures markets. A for-profit competitor has sprung up, Intrade in Ireland, whose location near Dublin allows it to operate legally. In the early 2000s, U.S. defense planners at the Pentagon briefly considered starting an event prediction market in terrorist events and assassinations, in the hope that a prediction market could provide an important new intelligence stream. However, the idea was deep-sixed, not least because it would provide market participants with some very distorted incentives. Media reaction was that the Pentagon's strategists were thinking so far outside the box that they were considering an option that was perhaps a bit crazy.

Still other strategists try to look at the future through the lens of cycle theories. Do you follow technical analysts in the equity markets or occasionally read books about multidecade Kondratiev waves? Personally I don't give too much credence to these attempts to make sense of the past and present on the assumption that patterns repeat endlessly, though there is one cycle that is very real of course: the business cycle, which was prematurely declared dead during the last boom. It is clearly shown that businesses and individuals overinvest, overspend, and overhype things during peaks, which tend to be frothy and speculative in mood, and then embrace an excessive pessimism during downturns—with the collective exaggeration amplifying swings.

Sri Lankan-born Canadian financier Sir Christopher Ondaatje points out that, if you are looking for something serious and interesting in the area of cycle theory, you could do worse that read Sir John Glubb's 1976 work on the fate of great countries, empires, and civilizations. Glubb Pasha (as he was usually known, given his title for having led the Arab Legion) took the view that such entities typically lasted about 250 years from their spirited origins to their final, clapped-out phases.

Glubb, as Sir Christopher points out and interprets, identifies a life cycle that begins with an Age of Pioneers ("an outburst of initiative, enterprise, courage and aggression"), continues with an Age of Conquests, and then an Age of Commerce. This "inevitably yields" to an Age of Affluence ("preoccupied with protecting . . . wealth and luxuries"); then there is an Age of Intellect ("dominated by endless discussion and debate") and finally an Age of Decadence ("marked by cynicism, frivolity"—"the heroes of the hour are athletes, singers and actors"). I'll admit that you don't have to buy into Glubb's cyclical notion in order to find something useful in his analysis.

Glubb thought in terms of complete 250-year intervals, and indeed time horizons are important: Some time ago I was talking with a friend on Wall Street about the business environment in 2015, but we were speaking past each other. I meant the year 2015, and he, using the 24-hour clock, was thinking in terms of the mood of the financial markets at 8:15 p.m. that night!

Envisioning the Future to Inform the Present

With the re-emergence of scenario planning as a critical tool for business leaders seeking to make sense of the complex drivers of global change and the implications they have for businesses, we at A.T. Kearney have happily been ahead of that curve. It's nothing new or exotic to us. In fact, we have employed scenario-based planning for over 20 years to help our clients explore how global trends might affect future business conditions. One of the many benefits of scenario planning is that it expands an individual's and an organization's field of vision, and helps them powerfully imagine the future.

The following is a set of scenario narratives that we generated recently for an internal partners meeting at A.T. Kearney. As is always the case with scenarios, our intention was not to predict the future. Rather, we were attempting to put forth engaging stories about the future (as our friends at Oxford University like to say) that could serve as a jumping-off point for robust discussion and strategic thinking. Our very bright and experienced Global Business Policy Council Managing Director, Erik Peterson, who joined us after stints at CSIS (the Center for Strategic and International Studies) and Kissinger Associates, created four scenarios titled: Terminus (a pessimistic scenario), Flatline (a base case), Top Gear (an optimistic, but possibly unrealistic scenario), and Control-Alt-Delete (a possibly more pausible optimistic scenario).

TOP GEAR

In Top Gear, economic authorities all over the world manage to get it right.

They coordinate to stimulate growth, reduce debt, shore up their financial institutions, and strengthen their competitiveness. The geographical scope of this global turnaround is stunning. In the United States, leaders manage to leave behind the partisanship that had paralyzed the policy process for so long. At once, they re-stimulate the economy and reduce the debt burden. A revived housing market, continued declines in unemployment, and a resurgence of investment contribute to restored consumer and market confidence. As a result, the economy returns to a 3 percent growth track by 2015.

The EU core countries make an historic commitment in 2014. After tremendous volatility in 2011 and 2012, they significantly expand the stabilization framework for the Eurozone in exchange for deep and lasting concessions from the periphery economies. New budget controls and fiscal mechanisms address the interlocking debt and financial crises that had embattled the euro. Support from China adds momentum to the turnaround. By 2015, the new system leads to economic vitality for the region as a whole. Aggregate trend growth rates for the EU exceed 2.5 percent for the 2015 to 2025 period. The recovery restores momentum to the integration agenda.

For its part, Beijing embarks on a major domestic transformation to moderate the breakneck pace of economic growth. It succeeds in strengthening domestic demand, reducing external surpluses, and pushing the country beyond the income trap of remaining a low-cost manufacturer. While highlighting the need to promote continued development and address income stratification in the thirteenth and fourteenth five-year development plans, China engineers a soft landing of moderate growth in the 7 percent range. The renminbi comes into a more realistic alignment with other major currencies.

In Japan, after more than a decade of economic anemia, the leadership succeeds in reinvigorating growth by aggressively removing failing companies and remaining financial bubbles. For its part, India addresses its physical infrastructure needs and removes bureaucratic barriers, adding to the momentum that it achieved in the early years of the twenty-first century. Its economy benefits from continued policy reforms, modernization of physical infrastructure, and overall improvements in the education of the Indian workforce.

Energy trends accelerate the economic revival. New discoveries of fossil fuels, the rapid development of unconventional gas, higher demand-side efficiencies, and continued innovations in alternative technologies all generate a lower-cost and more stable energy outlook.

Global economic dynamism extends to Africa, Latin America, and the Middle East, which continues to go through a political and social redefinition triggered by the Arab Spring in 2011.

This dramatic turnaround in key economies translates into trend global output growth of well over 5 percent. This means better lives, higher prosperity, a growing middle class, and more opportunity the world over. Any one of these contingencies by itself would be significant. All of them together represent what we call Top Gear—the alignment of the stars that serves to restore growth and prosperity worldwide.

TERMINUS

In Terminus, things simply unravel.

In the context of protracted economic and financial instability and anemic global growth, leaders are incapable of sustaining support for the globalization that has shaped the economic and business environment for decades. No matter how compelling the economic and financial logic, the politics of procrastination and recalcitrance cannot be overcome. The collapse of the Papandreou government in Greece in 2011 triggers cascading failures in periphery and core euro economies.

One political figure after the next is pushed from power.

In their place emerges a class of leaders who can and do say "no" to austerity and reform but have no viable alternative vision. Defaults in two periphery economies throw the region into tumult. This fragmentation generates crippling levels of unemployment and dislocation. Protests in Athens, Rome, Madrid, and Frankfurt become increasingly destructive.

Things are little different in the United States. Dragged down by a mounting debt overhang, Washington resorts to blatantly protectionist legislation forced through Congress by the newly elected political extreme. The actions set off retaliatory policies in Brussels and Beijing. Trade flows decline precipitously amid escalating allegations of trade practices that are regarded as predatory and illegal. Once again, U.S. international financial and economic ratings are downgraded. Vacillating calls for isolationism and aggressive engagement marks the resulting downward spiral.

The ensuing economic downturn has explosive social effects. Populism runs rampant. In both the United States and Europe, the Occupy movement that began in 2011 intensifies, and the tempo of these demonstrations increases. They agitate in different places and in different languages, but everywhere the message is the same: "We are the 99 percent!" The key rallying point across geographies is widespread resentment of inequality, greed, lack of opportunity, and disenfranchisement. In response to sharply higher unemployment, the spotlight shifts to immigrants who are perceived as taking away jobs. "Retaking our country" becomes the political battle cry of extremist political parties and groups in various countries.

China must face the sharp decline of its export markets in the United States and Europe. The leadership in Beijing encounters serious pressures from income inequality, corruption, sluggish domestic demand, and rampant environmental degradation. While the leadership proclaims the superiority of the Chinese model, the country retreats into a strategy of defensive economic consolidation.

The global economy falls into a protracted funk at or around the 0 percent growth level. The process of globalization unwinds, and countries concentrate on economic security as a way to avoid foreign entanglements. Competition for global resources, however, brings the largest economies into conflict. The age of resource geopolitics has arrived in full force.

Terminus is the end of the line for globalization as we have known it. In its place arises a set of defensive, inward-looking national policies.

FLATLINE

In Flatline, global leaders cannot extricate their countries from the 2011 to 2012 recession, resulting in an extended period of acute economic anemia. The entire world economy declines to a 10-year trend rate of 2.5 percent from 2015 to 2025. Compared with previous trend growth of 4.1 percent, foregone economic output reaches $28.2 trillion by 2025.

In the United States, efforts to bridge the prevailing political philosophies fall short. Sharp partisanship after the 2012 presidential election contributes to additional declines in confidence and lack of trust in government. The economic challenges confronting the country—continued high unemployment, an ailing housing sector, depressed business and consumer confidence, and political paralysis—create a combustible mix that forestalls hopes for a recovery. In the meantime, a growing retired population of politically assertive Baby Boomers, mounting healthcare and retirement costs, degraded physical infrastructure, and a dysfunctional educational system all chip away at the country's competitiveness. In the economic and commercial funk that follows, public debt levels reach 100 percent of GDP by 2018, and GDP growth stalls at 1 percent.

Things are no more encouraging in Europe, where countries are unable to provide a lasting, structural response to the cascading and ever more severe debt crises. Rather than seeking bold solutions, European political leaders kick the can down the road, just like their counterparts in the United States. What follows is a protracted period of high instability and low growth. Below-average eurozone growth of 1 percent results in a stuttering, multi-speed Europe that has reached the limits of integration. Germany especially is subject to rising and potent public opposition to what is characterized as a transfer union.

In Russia, it is a more-of-the-same proposition. Buoyed by revenue from oil and natural gas exports, the country continues its on-again, off-again efforts to avert the natural resource curse by developing capabilities in research and development and innovation. In Japan, despite the minor growth resulting from the 2011 to 2012 reconstruction programs, fundamental issues are not addressed. As a result, Tokyo continues to be unable to restart its growth engine.

The economic anemia spreads to high-growth developing economies, most notably China and India, where growth rates drop to 6 percent and 5 percent respectively due to the collapse of export markets to the West.

The economic slowdown amplifies political and social pressures in both countries. The challenge is especially pronounced in Beijing, where leaders face relentless political and social pressures to combat poverty and maintain growth and opportunity. Still, the BRICs continue to represent the engine of the global economy. The output gap between the developing and developed worlds continues to widen.

The Middle East moves through a protracted period of political and economic instability associated with the Arab Spring. While key countries were able to remove the regimes they did not want, they cannot agree on what future they do want.

Flatline illustrates the simultaneous failure of leadership in key countries across the planet. It is a story about deferred actions, lack of leadership, self-inflicted wounds, and a highly uncertain business environment.

CONTROL-ALT-DELETE

In Control-Alt-Delete, it gets much worse before it gets much better.

Dragged down by aging populations, a loss of competitiveness, and widening societal fissures, the United States and Europe reach critical political and economic inflection points in 2018.

It takes a second recession, festering political recalcitrance, a more threatening geopolitical environment, and mounting social unrest to get there. The instability starts in Europe, where political leaders can no longer cope with the challenges they face. Riots break out in cities across Europe, as parts of the Occupy movement turn violent. The demonstrations serve as a rallying point for disjointed causes, including youth demonstrations agitating for intergenerational equity, immigrants pushing for rights, and unions whose members are squeezed by historically high levels of unemployment.

Circumstances in the United States are similar. Leaders struggle with continued high unemployment, declining competitiveness, and an overwhelming lack of trust in the government. Increasingly strident voices elected in 2012 call for nationalist responses to the country's deepening problems. The political discourse is marked by even more aggressive partisanship. The drumbeat of demonstrations intensifies. Pervasive social networking and flash mobbing feed the growth of these movements on both sides of the Atlantic.

The situation deteriorates in other areas of the world as well. After the second recession, Beijing mounts an even more aggressive global campaign to secure critical resources. This includes the so-called land grab—efforts to gain control of agriculture, energy, and water in Africa, the Middle East, and Latin America. Russia continues to struggle with a lackluster economy, low competitiveness, and a sharply declining population. Revenue from the country's energy and other raw-material exports continues to be channeled to the military. Moscow gradually rebuilds its capacity to project power outside its borders.

In the face of this deteriorating economic, social, and geopolitical outlook, leaders in the West manage to rise to the challenge. 2018 becomes the global reset point—the control-alt-delete reboot. It marks a fundamental shift in the respective pathways of the United States and Europe.

In the United States, leaders are able to find common ground. They retool the federal budget system; enact major reforms on education, health care, and physical infrastructure; and put into place a bold plan to reduce the country's debt obligations. Restored consumer and market confidence result in renewed economic growth.

Europe also regains momentum. Thanks to an historic commitment between the EU's core and periphery countries, economic and financial stability is strengthened considerably. A number of next-generation political parties are swept into power on platforms of equity, fiscal responsibility, and sustainable economic growth. The national and EU agendas are retooled to account for this shift in core attitudes. What follows is the onset of the political and economic redefinition of Europe.

The turnarounds in the United States and Europe reinforce equally positive shifts in other countries that benefit from higher trade and investment flows. Global economic growth reaches the 5 percent level.

Control-Alt-Delete is a back-from-the-brink story that ends well.

The Coming Chinese Commonwealth?

Thinking a bit further ahead, there are things scenario planners call predetermined elements—and they are sometimes far more important than the out-of-the-blue wildcards and black swans, for they are about largely unstoppable megatrends that are truly mega. The most obvious example of a predetermined element in our era is the rise of China as an economic, political, and military superpower—something that is curiously both well-known and poorly understood.

My good friend Josef "Joe" Joffe of Hamburg, who combines the editor and publisher role at one of Germany's most prestigious newspapers (*Die Zeit*) with a part-time academic appointment at Stanford, has carefully studied periods in history when new powers rise. It's delicate, and indeed dangerous, as the existing players must learn to accommodate the new powers, while the rising stars must learn to use their new strengths responsibly and for the common good of the world. Joe likes to call this last bit "teenage driver's syndrome": New powers like to flex their newly developed muscles, and sometimes the result is a serious accident.

What's dangerous about all this is that we, as human beings, don't have a very good track record. The great rising powers of the early twentieth century were Imperial Germany and Imperial Japan. The status-quo powers did not work especially hard to accommodate them and integrate them smoothly into the world system, and likewise Germany and Japan did not always use their new strengths responsibly. The overall results included two world wars, a hundred million (or more) deaths, and wreckage that is still with us in parts of the world.

With regard to China's rise, let's hope we can all learn from these lessons of history. As I mentioned earlier in the book, China fully intends to be a superpower in all respects, including in military hard-power terms. China's 2005 Taiwan Anti-Secession Law commits China to war in the event Taiwan pursues or declares independence. (Curiously, the leadership in Beijing is fine with Taiwan's polite fiction of calling itself the Republic of China on Taiwan and claiming to be the rightful government of all of China, something that few Taiwanese feel strongly about anymore.) Under more ambiguous terms, the United States has a treaty commitment to defend Taiwan. Of course, nobody wants war, but sometimes things escalate, and miscalculations or mistakes happen.

So I would like to put forward a more hopeful scenario for the 2030 to 2050 time range in Asia: that China is an increasingly rich, productive, influential, and collaborative superpower, taking responsibility not only for its own interests but also for the peace and prosperity of the world as a whole, in cooperation with the United States, Europe, India, Russia, Brazil, Canada, Australia, and the other major players. Just as a shrewd formula was found to allow Hong Kong to maintain its liberties and rule of law—one country, two systems—I can imagine that new formulae will be found to accommodate Taiwan. One can even picture the revival of the primordial dragon symbol as the banner of a new Chinese Commonwealth, which could include associated countries such as Singapore. I realize these are mere speculations, but unless we have a vision of the future that we are working toward, the future will be less of a destination and more of a crapshoot.

Yes, there are some terrifying risks, but, on the other hand, there is the immense power of human ingenuity and resilience. No matter how dark things looked in the 1930s and 1940s, the sun did shine again. Despite the crisis-filled headlines, did you know that the evidence shows that the world is actually getting less violent? (If you don't believe this, check out Harvard professor Steven Pinker's statistical analysis.) Oh, and are you ready for the next robust recovery—or boom? For boom it will again. As I've said before, we tend to overestimate the impact of technological advances in the short run, but underestimate it in the long run. Down the road, technologically speaking, things look very bright—even downright exciting.

> *As I've said before, we tend to overestimate the impact of technological advances in the short run, but underestimate it in the long run. Down the road, technologically speaking, things look very bright—even downright exciting.*

Executives don't have the luxury of staying on the sidelines. They must act, and they must invest. That's a good thing. Also on the positive side, beyond scientific and technological advances, there is the civilizing force of middle-class prosperity that is now reaching increasing hundreds of millions (and in time eventually billions) of people. In the twentieth century, regeneration after war and upheaval went hand in hand with the power of free markets and free ideas. These days, we mostly remember the unpleasant surprises of the past decade or so (from 9/11 and the Middle East wars to the global financial crisis). But it's worth remembering that in the mid-1980s, very few of us imagined that the fall of the Berlin wall was just around the corner—opening up new frontiers and breathing new life into dozens of countries.

Pulling It All Together and Getting Ready to Beat the Global Odds

If you've stayed with me this long, you know the many ways in which it's become a really topsy-turvy world out there—and getting ever faster, bumpier, and more complex with each passing day. But it's also a world brimming over with new opportunities (and, indeed, new hope) for those ready to chart a new course. Farsighted entrepreneurs and innovators have gotten right on with bringing simplicity, delight, and a lighter use of materials and energy to whatever they do (with the ever-greater complexity inside hidden away from the human eye and brain). The onrush of new technology and terabytes of new information—at times the source of today's sense of overload and frazzle—now offer more promise than ever for helping us sort out the critical information wheat from the data chaff.

As I've counseled in this book (and I've taken my own medicine), we all need to try to steer carefully to avoid the two bipolar extremes of wait-and-see inaction and frenzied hyperactivity. In order to find that creative mean, we need to take time regularly to pause, to clarify our thinking and strategies, and to critically examine our assumptions (especially those that happen to mirror whatever today's herd-mentality, common wisdom happens to be). And we need to become omnivores, too: Vary your information diet, and personally go out in the world to check out remarkable emerging people, ideas, places, products, and services for yourself. Of course relationships and core values matter more than ever in this epoch of broken bonds of trust, so never confuse a mere connection or transaction with a real relationship—though many long-lasting relationships may nowadays begin as contacts or transaction counter-parties.

Then it's time to get moving. Armed with fresh clarity, ideas, passion, and conviction, you and I can seize new opportunities without having to wait for that perfect data set. What really helps is learning to think in terms of scenarios, as we naturally crave exact forecasts (and the illusion of certainty). Scenario thinking opens us up to a range of new possibilities that we never before considered, and it also forces us to be skeptical of our usual sources. Taken together, these approaches create the basis for principled, decisive action that creates lasting value—and that's how you can beat the global odds.

Epilogue

The Next Chapter

O ver the past six years of my tenure as chairman and managing partner of A.T. Kearney, I have had the honor of leading the transformation of the firm by opening up an aperture to new sources of growth and value and also by reaffirming the unwavering principles guiding the firm, which were embraced some 86 years ago by our late founder, Tom Kearney. Tom was one of the early pioneers in management consulting, and he and James O. "Mac" McKinsey became business partners in the late 1920s—the former in Chicago and the latter in New York. For a time, there was even a firm called McKinsey, Kearney & Co. But in the years after "Mac" died, Tom's Chicago office became the independent firm A.T. Kearney. For decades, the firm enjoyed solid growth, with successive generations of partners embracing and carrying forth the authentic values that are quintessentially "A.T. Kearney."

A.T. Kearney was owned by EDS from 1995 to early 2006. It became a difficult relationship during the later years; A.T. Kearney's performance suffered and the firm risked losing its sense of identity. We, the partners, rather courageously bought the fragile firm back, nursed it to health, and even managed to pay off our debt in one year's time. The firm's partners elected me to my current position a few short months after the buyout.

With our firm's important (and inspiring) history in mind, I took our partners and employees on a values-based visioning exercise designed to inspire commitment and leadership and enable success by delivering on the needs of clients and stakeholders with a forward-thinking orientation. This was fundamentally an outside-in look, employing all the tools of scenario-based planning to discern the signs of change and to manage them appropriately in order to best define and meet the needs of our clients and one another.

As I mentioned earlier, this has sometimes, even early on, required making difficult decisions: among them the need to remove some of the firm's highest commercial performers who, despite their worldly success, were insufficiently committed to our values and standards. Although I received much advice to the contrary, removing these individuals reaffirmed the firm's dedication to values central to its culture and legacy. It also very quickly released pent-up energy from those colleagues who recommitted themselves to a firm that they believed had reaffirmed its distinctive value proposition and culture.

And despite the deep recession we faced in recent years, we also decided against any wholesale cut in our headcount. Of course, it's widely accepted that significant layoffs are an essential and standard operating procedure in tough times. But that was, in my view, a course that would only boost our profits in the short run at the expense of our competitive position over time. As a friend of mine likes to say, "You can't shrink your way to greatness."

In fact, I believe we managed to defy the paradox of time and space by actually expanding our global presence during the downturn (thereby resisting the restraints of space), and by investing in new lines of business, new areas of expertise, and in the development of our people, despite the often inexorable urge to manage to the bottom line (thereby resisting the restraints of time). With this forward-thinking, values-based leadership, we navigated the firm to double-digit growth, extraordinarily strong employee engagement, and brand resurgence.

We've grown throughout the worst market conditions since the Great Depression (the era, by the way, in which A.T. Kearney originally established itself as a management consulting pioneer). In fact, since the management buyout in 2006, we've grown from 46 offices in 30 countries to 57 offices in 39 countries. And the firm is now poised to seize its growing ambitions with an even more robust escape velocity.

All this has been made possible by walking the talk of this book. We followed a rigorous process of broad-gauged, forward-thinking leadership grounded in a values-based, collaborative, and inclusive culture. Our actions were anchored in rich relationships able to deliver immediate impact and drive growing advantage for our clients and one another. At every step, these actions were consistent with the best interests of the larger communities of stakeholders affected by all our decisions—commercial, governmental, and personal.

As I turn to my next personal journey with my tenure as chairman and managing partner winding down, I ready myself to find a new way of weaving together my three life journeys—contemplative (the seminary); policy (government—the U.N., U.S. Senate, and Overseas Development Council); and commercial (Mobil, SRI International, and A.T. Kearney)—in order to apply intellect, insight, and inspiration to guide my future ambitions and actions. Having contributed to the transformation of A.T. Kearney and now having paused to distill the essence of it all, I look forward to the future with a renewed excitement and sense of the possible. My hope is that in some small way this account of my journey might help you, the reader, create a future with a compelling sense of perspective, passion, and purpose.

Afterword

The final chapter of this book, in charting four possible futures for the world, was quite a roller-coaster ride. But it was an authentic one: The spectrum of human futures indeed ranges from the bleak to the bright—or, to adopt the nomenclature of that last chapter, from "Terminus" to "Top Gear."

If you ask what it will take to get the brighter, globally prosperous outcome, you find yourself underscoring a central theme of this book: There is a connection between the moral—you might even say spiritual—and the pragmatically commercial. More often than not, the way to do well is to do some good along the way. Indeed, my own view is that if the world is going to make the economic and political progress envisioned in the Top Gear scenario, it will have to make moral progress as well.

For example, the Top Gear scenario envisions European nations cooperating to achieve an expanded stabilization framework. This would indeed be helpful, in keeping with the common view that for the European Union to sustain its economic integration, its political integration will have to grow.

But for that to happen, Europeans will have to draw on the better angels of their nature. They'll have to resist the tribalistic impulses of raw nationalism and work to see each other's point of view. People in Germany will have to put themselves in the shoes of people in Ireland or Spain, and vice versa. This sort of "perspective taking" is often vital to solving non-zero-sum problems and getting to a win-win, value-creating outcome, and in the case of European integration, it's particularly challenging because it involves overcoming impediments that are deeply ingrained in human nature.

For example, for the richer and poorer nations of Europe to collaborate, both groups will have to overcome resentment—the rich's resentment of the so-called freeloaders who need assistance and the poor's resentment of the influence (that is, the strings attached) that tends to come with assistance. To overcome these natural resentments takes real work, an earnest attempt to put yourself in the shoes of the other and thus understand the perspective from which an otherwise grating policy position makes sense.

I like to refer to this broadening of perspective as "moral imagination"—not only because I consider it good to ponder perspectives other than your own, but because doing this so often leads to good outcomes, to those win-win solutions to non-zero-sum games. In Europe, getting to the Top Gear scenario will call for people to expand their moral imaginations across borders of nation, language, ethnicity, and class. Obviously, European history is littered with zero-sum, win-lose outcomes, and for that matter, with lose-lose outcomes to non-zero-sum games. There have been flagrant land grabs and long, mutually destructive wars. Happily, the current extent of economic interdependence makes a regression to such belligerence unlikely, but even so, we've got a way to go before we reach the levels of mutual understanding needed to successfully confront today's serial crises.

It isn't just these grand bargains of economic policy that have a moral dimension; the everyday business of the modern executive does, too. To do high-level commercial collaboration across national boundaries is to engage in cultural interchange, to symmetrically expand horizons. When you play a non-zero-sum game with "the other"— someone in a different social circumstance than yours—and play it to a win–win outcome, you'll probably come to appreciate the perspective on the other side of the border a bit better. And in so doing, you've strengthened, by at least a little, the global social fabric.

Expanding our moral imaginations, in addition to being a prerequisite for a bright future, is a happy by-product of some of the advice Paul Laudicina has shared with us in this book. He counsels: "Vary your information diet, and go out in the world *personally* to check out remarkable emerging people, ideas, places, products, and services for yourself." You can't do a truly good job of that without enlarging your perspective across boundaries of culture, nation, language, and class.

Paul also warns against the temptation to make all our commercial relationships merely transactional. *Real* relationships—as opposed to mere connections—"matter more than ever in this epoch of broken bonds of trust." This is good practical advice, but it's also another case where doing the practical means doing the moral, even the spiritual. When you establish an enduring bond across cultural, national, or socioeconomic lines, you're, so to speak, doing God's work.

This book has emphasized nothing more strongly than the importance of getting the big picture—stepping back and seeing the broader forces at work, notably the interplay between greater complexity and greater connectedness. And the book practices what it preaches; it has made the case for the big picture by stepping back and getting the big picture. So it is thoroughly in the spirit of this book if I try to zoom out further still. I want to shed some light on how far back the roots of this complex, connected world go.

It's possible to see globalized society as a fairly straightforward outgrowth of primordial society. Ever since the Stone Age, people have been inventing things—the wheel, writing, money—that have expanded the potential scope of social organization.

To put it more abstractly: These inventions have made it possible to play non-zero-sum games, games with win–win or lose–lose outcomes, at greater and greater distances with more and more people. This inexorable growth in information, transportation, and other technologies has been a key driver of the expansion and complexification of social organization—from hunter-gatherer band to multivillage tribe to city-state to state, and so on.

And this expanded social structure has brought moral progress—it has led people to expand their definition of community to encompass more and more kinds of people. There was a time when members of one Greek city-state considered members of another Greek city-state subhuman. Then, as social organization grew to encompass Greece broadly, the idea that all Greeks are human took root.

Of course, this perspective fell short of complete moral enlightenment. According to Plutarch, Aristotle advised Alexander the Great to treat all Greeks as humans but to treat non-Greeks "as though they were plants or animals." Still, there was more progress to come. Today, in the more cosmopolitan parts of the world, it goes without saying that all people, regardless of race, nationality, religion, or gender, are fully human, deserving of full human rights.

And I think it's no coincidence that these cosmopolitan parts of the world tend to be among the more commercially advanced parts of the world. That's because there is indeed a link between doing well and doing good; in an economically intertwined world, intolerance is, in addition to bad manners, bad business.

I think this kind of link between doing good and doing well is particularly crucial now because of precisely where we are in humankind's cosmic journey. That trajectory of societal evolution—from band to tribe to state, and so on—has gotten us to the brink of a globalized society. But only the brink. What we call "global society" doesn't have the order and stability that we often associate with the word *society*. And acquiring that sort of stable coherence is hardly assured.

History tells us as much. Whole civilizations have collapsed, again and again and again. Sure, in the longest run, recovery has tended to ensue, and eventually civilization reaches a higher level than its precollapse level. But that's little consolation to the people who endure years or even decades of poverty, chaos, and/or slaughter. Those four scenarios—from Top Gear all the way to Terminus—should all be taken seriously.

What will it take to avert Terminus? Two things, I think. One is at the level of policy. The challenges facing the European Union are in a sense a microcosm of the challenges facing the whole world. They are just a particular case where the filaments of public policy need to cross borders to solve non-zero-sum problems faced by many nations. In some cases this has already started; the World Trade Organization, by adjudicating trade disputes, has done a passable job of keeping protectionism at bay. In other cases there has been little or no progress. An international treaty that could successfully inhibit cyber attacks would be nice, for example. So would a biological weapons convention with teeth.

Solving public policy problems on this scale may sound like a daunting challenge—and it is—but the good news is that money is on the side of success; if the forces of global capitalism are enlightened, they will abet the evolution of global governance because capitalism thrives best on a stable platform.

History offers some encouragement here. Commerce has often, one way or another, managed to make the world safe for itself. In the late Middle Ages, merchants in various German cities united to form the Hanseatic League so that they could quell pirates and build light-houses. At about the same time, kings across Europe grabbed power from local lords, paving the way for the nation-state—and they did so as proxies for the incipient capitalist system. The conflicting regulations of the various lords had been impeding commerce, and lords had been fighting one another and even marauding, thus making trade perilous. The emerging merchant middle class gladly paid taxes to ascendant kings in exchange for peace and order.

In both cases, commerce's drive for self-preservation carried gov-ernance to a higher level of organization—from the local to the regional. And in both cases, this was because commerce at that higher level was threatened. Maybe we can hope for comparable action from today's capitalists—not just in the European Union but around the world.

Here is what world history would look like if you turned the past 10,000 years into a 10-minute time-lapse film: an expanding web of economic interaction that entailed expanding social organization and expanding realms of governance. And if you looked closely at the texture of this social fabric, you would see two themes that Paul's book has dealt with so acutely and wisely: the aforementioned growing complexity and growing connectedness.

The two are of course related. Growing social complexity to a large extent *consists* of us being connected to more and more people. This is a blessing and a curse. The blessing is one of efficiency; the Internet, by connecting us to so many different people, allows us to play more non-zero-sum games, to do more business, and to create more prosperity than was possible 50 years ago. But the flip side is that the average connection, compared to the average connection of 50 years ago, is superficial; we find ourselves interacting with people along the dimension that the transaction of the moment demands, and as a result never get to know the whole person.

Paul has argued that though we of course have to exploit the efficiencies offered by the new technologies, we shouldn't get lost in them. We must sometimes make a point of turning one-dimensional relationships into three-dimensional ones; we ought to view people not as just nodes in the giant social brain we're all part of, but as people; and we must every once in a while step out of the information cocoon that the most narrowly pragmatic conception of our work would have us weave for ourselves.

It makes sense to me. After all, if we spend all our time as ruthlessly efficient information processors, as neurons in the burgeoning global brain, we'll never get to pause and see the brain that's being built. If we want to master the system we're part of, rather than be mastered by it, we have to sometimes step outside of it and even defy its dictates. This is just good pragmatic advice. What a happy coincidence that it's advice that will also enrich us as human beings and as moral beings.

Robert Wright
Senior Future Tense Fellow, New America Foundation, and
Contributing Editor, *The Atlantic*

Selected Bibliography

Adamson, Allen P. *BrandSimple: How the Best Brands Keep It Simple and Succeed.* New York: Palgrave Macmillan, 2006.

Arthur, W. Brian. *The Nature of Technology: What It Is and How It Evolves.* New York: Free Press, 2009.

Attali, Jacques. *A Brief History of the Future.* New York: Arcade Publishing, 2009.

Bahrami, Homa, and Stuart Evans. *Super-Flexibility for Knowledge Enterprises: A Toolkit for Dynamic Adaptation.* Heidelberg: Springer, 2010.

Bobbitt, Philip. *Terror and Consent: The Wars for the Twenty-First Century.* New York: Knopf, 2008.

Cashman, Kevin. *The Pause Principle: Step Back to Lead Forward.* San Francisco: Berrett-Koehler, 2012.

Coggan, Philip. *Paper Promises: Money, Debt and the New World Order.* London: Allen Lane, 2011.

Collini, Stefan. *What Are Universities For?* London: Penguin, 2012.

Cooper, Thomas W. *Fast Media Media Fast: How to Clear Your Mind and Invigorate Your Life in the Age of Media Overload.* Boulder, CO: Gaeta Press, 2011.

Cowen, Tyler. *The Great Stagnation: How America Ate All the Low-Hanging Fruit of Modern History, Got Sick, and Will (Eventually) Feel Better.* New York: Dutton Adult, 2011.

Diamandis, Peter H., and Steven Kotler. *Abundance: The Future Is Better Than You Think.* New York: Free Press, 2012.

Edwards, Sebastian. *Left Behind: Latin America and the False Promise of Populism.* Chicago: University of Chicago Press, 2010.

Ferguson, Niall. *Civilization: The Six Ways the West Beat the Rest.* London: Allen Lane, 2011.

Florida, Richard. *The Great Reset: How the Post-Crash Economy Will Change the Way We Live and Work.* New York: Harper, 2010.

Fukuyama, Francis. *The Origins of Political Order: From Prehuman Times to the French Revolution.* New York: Farrar, Straus & Giroux, 2011.

Gardner, Dan. *Future Babble: Why Expert Predictions Are Next to Worthless, and You Can Do Better.* New York: Dutton, 2011.

Garon, Sheldon. *Beyond Our Means: Why America Spends While the World Saves.* Princeton, NJ: Princeton University Press, 2012.

Gershenfeld, Neil. *Fab: The Coming Revolution on Your Desktop—From Personal Computers to Personal Fabrication.* New York: Basic Books, 2007.

Guest, Robert. *Borderless Economics: Chinese Sea Turtles, Indian Fridges and the New Fruits of Global Capitalism.* New York: Palgrave Macmillan, 2011.

Hale, David, and Lyric Hughes Hale. *What's Next: Unconventional Wisdom on the Future of the World Economy.* New Haven, CT: Yale University Press, 2011.

Hoffman, Reid, and Ben Casnocha. *The Start-Up of You: Adapt to the Future, Invest in Yourself, and Transform Your Career.* New York: Crown Business, 2012.

Holstein, William J. *The Next American Economy: Blueprint for a Real Recovery.* New York: Walker & Co., 2011.

Joffe, Josef. *Predictions: The Future of the Great Powers.* London: Phoenix, 1998.

Johnson, Clay A. *The Information Diet: A Case for Conscious Consumption.* Sebastopol, CA: O'Reilly, 2012.

Johnson, Steven. *Where Good Ideas Come From: The Natural History of Innovation.* New York: Riverhead Books, 2010.

Kahneman, Daniel. *Thinking, Fast and Slow.* New York: Farrar, Straus & Giroux, 2011.

Kotkin, Joel. *The Next Hundred Million: America in 2050.* New York: Penguin, 2010.

Levinson, Marc. *The Box: How the Shipping Container Made the World Smaller and the World Economy Bigger.* Princeton, NJ: Princeton University Press, 2008.

Prince Hans-Adam II of Liechtenstein. *The State in the Third Millennium.* Triesen, Liechtenstein: Van Eck Publishers, 2009.

MacKay, Charles. *Extraordinary Popular Delusions and the Madness of Crowds.* Various editions since 1841.

Mahbubani, Kishore. *The New Asian Hemisphere: The Irresistible Shift of Global Power to the East.* New York: PublicAffairs, 2008.

Mason, Paul. *Why It's Kicking Off Everywhere: The New Global Revolutions.* London and New York: Verso, 2012.

Morozov, Evgeny. *The Net Delusion: The Dark Side of Internet Freedom.* New York: Public Affairs, 2011.

Naím, Moisés. *Illicit: How Smugglers, Traffickers, and Copycats Are Hijacking the Global Economy*. New York: Anchor, 2006.

Ondaatje, Sir Christopher. *The Power of Paper: A History, a Financial Adventure and a Warning*. London: HarperCollins, 2007.

Patten, Chris (Lord Patten of Barnes). *What Next? Surviving the Twenty-First Century*. London: Allen Lane, 2008.

Perlow, Leslie A. *Sleeping with Your Smartphone: How to Break the 24/7 Habit and Change the Way You Work*. Boston: Harvard Business Review Press, 2012.

Poscente, Vince. *The Age of Speed: Learning to Thrive in a More-Faster-Now World*. Austin: Bard Press, 2008.

Quelch, John A., and Katherine E. Jocz. *All Business Is Local: Why Place Matters More Than Ever in a Global, Virtual World*. New York: Portfolio/Penguin, 2012.

Roberts, Kevin. *Lovemarks: The Future Beyond Brands*. New York: PowerHouse Books, 2005.

Rodrik, Dani. *The Globalization Paradox: Democracy and the Future of the World Economy*. New York: W.W. Norton, 2011.

Schwartz, Barry. *The Paradox of Choice: Why More Is Less*. New York: Harper Perennial, 2005.

Wade, Woody. *Scenario Planning: A Field Guide to the Future*. New York: Wiley, 2012.

Wallis, Jim. *Rediscovering Values: On Wall Street, Main Street, and Your Street*. New York: Howard Books, 2010.

Wilson, Daniel H. *Where's My Jetpack? A Guide to the Amazing Science Fiction Future That Never Arrived*. New York: Bloomsbury, 2007.

Wright, Robert. *Nonzero: The Logic of Human Destiny*. New York: Vintage, 2001.

Yergin, Daniel. *The Quest: Energy, Security, and the Remaking of the Modern World*. New York: Penguin, 2011.

Acknowledgments

This book is as much about seeking a personal path through the thicket of information overload and frenetic activity of our modern world as it is about helping the reader find sanity and clarity in the midst of our technology-dominated lives that increasingly respect no boundaries.

But in the process of seeking to cut a path through the jungle of a demanding life, I am afraid I have offloaded many of the critical personal demands on my time to those closest to me—my wife, children, and friends. So as I bring an important chapter of my life to a close and get ready to start a new one, I pause to thank them profoundly for generously excusing me from all those important daily demands on time and attention that would have delayed, if not deprived me of, the insights central to the experience that illuminates this book. To my wife, Louise, and four children—Chris, Lee, Carla, and Nikki—I say, "Thank you." I also want to assure them that I will take my own medicine and be back, focused with clarity and purpose on those priorities that should rightly be at the center of everyone's life.

I am also deeply indebted to my leadership team at A.T. Kearney that has so ably and loyally helped steer our firm off the early post-MBO shoals to the fair winds of strong, sustainable performance. You have made it easy for me to take the lead, effectively orchestrating the respective talents of our team to gain the trust and confidence of the whole global A.T. Kearney family of clients and colleagues. And to that family of colleagues across the network of 57 offices in 39 countries around the world who have so generously made good on our promises to our clients and to one another, thank you for giving me the privilege of leading you these last six years as we have successfully fought to beat the global odds of a most challenging business environment.

Finally, any piece of intellectual capital is always the product of countless stimuli from people and places often too numerous and varied to even recall. That is certainly true of this book, which cites explicitly the insights of many individuals who have helped unlock some of the mysteries and paradoxes that I explore in these pages.

Among those I need to emphatically acknowledge are the many clients who allowed me the privilege of gaining insight into their special needs and patiently permitted me to help them address these needs. I have, over the years, benefitted from numerous client relationships that have transformed into friendships with extraordinarily talented and dedicated leaders of industry and government literally across the four corners of the globe. The benefits of these relationships have been so rich, varied, and mutual as to render indistinguishable the notion of client/consultant. In addition, from my many years at the helm of the Global Business Policy Council of A.T. Kearney, I have had the enviable opportunity to engage and learn from the best and the brightest from every walk of life—satisfying my insatiable need to develop the kind of peripheral vision that this book is all about.

However, there are a few individuals who have played an especially important role in helping me tell this story and bring it to the global marketplace of ideas. To the extent that my thesis is cogent, compelling, and in print, they are largely responsible. My sincere thanks go to my literary agent, Rafe Sagalyn; editors Evan Burton and Emilie Herman and the entire John Wiley & Sons team; my publicist, Angela Hayes; and Bart Crosby and the Crosby Associates team for their diligent and creative work in helping illustrate the book's ideas with compelling visual images, assisted by A.T. Kearney's own artistic and marketing talent provided by Kevin Peschke, Doug MacDonald, and Lee Anne Petry.

My executive assistant, Patty Fabian, has been the ringmaster of the many claimants on my time, providing discipline and boundaries central to my thinking and sanity. I am grateful for the ballast she has brought to my professional life over the past 11 years.

The critical and timely support of my special assistant, Justin Shepherd, has not only helped me juggle my day job demands at the helm of A.T. Kearney, but has also provided the added (and rare) bonus of offering special intellectual insight reflected in my thinking and decisions as well as in very important ways for the preparation of this book. I also wish to acknowledge the diligent research assistance support of Dillon Forrest.

Finally, there is one person who has been on this intellectual and professional journey with me longer than anyone. My former colleague, intellectual soulmate, and fellow Santa Fean Stephen Klimczuk played a central role in the preparation of this book. Without his tireless, focused, talented, and dedicated support of this book project—much as was the case with my last book, *World Out of Balance*—this manuscript would not be in print.

To all those I cite in this book and to the many unacknowledged others who have touched my life along the way and helped shape my thoughts and values, I offer my profound thanks.

P.A.L.

About the Author

Paul Laudicina is the CEO, chairman of the board, and managing partner at global management-consulting firm A.T. Kearney, and the founder and chairman of the firm's Global Business Policy Council. He has more than 40 years of professional experience in various capacities in government, research institutions, businesses, and the United Nations and has worked in over 30 countries at the national, provincial, state, and community levels.

With more than 25 years of global consulting experience, Paul has worked with leaders of corporations and governments across a broad range of strategic, corporate, and public policy issues. He has also led scenario-based strategic planning and risk-management engagements for many of A.T. Kearney's largest private- and public-sector clients.

In early 2006, the Partners of A.T. Kearney elected Paul to lead the firm following its management buy-out, and under his leadership the firm has strongly rebounded to retake its place among the world's leading management consulting firms, returning to robust growth and retiring its debt within a year of regaining independence. Prior to the MBO, A.T. Kearney had been an EDS subsidiary for over a decade, and the relationship with the parent had become strained and this storied, pioneering consulting firm was in serious trouble. Some six years later, A.T. Kearney is one of the great turnaround stories of the professional services sector, with strong growth fuelled by global expansion, a differentiated brand identity, and client satisfaction and employee loyalty scores that have enabled it to reclaim its place as an industry leader.

Before joining A.T. Kearney in 1991, Paul was senior vice president and director with SRI International, the former Stanford Research Institute, where he was employed for 10 years. He is also the founder of its policy division. He had earlier served as legislative director to then U.S. Senator Joseph R. Biden Jr.; director of preinvestment studies for Mobil Corporation; associate fellow of the Overseas Development Council; and research associate for the United Nations' Center for Economic and Social Information. In that role, he worked domestically and in Latin America, Switzerland, and East Africa.

Paul is the author of a number of articles and books, including *World Out of Balance: Navigating Global Risks to Seize Competitive Advantage*, which was published in six additional language editions and was selected as one of the top business books of 2005 by Soundview Executive Book Summaries. He was also named to *Consulting* magazine's annual ranking of the Top 25 Most Influential Consultants in 2005 and 2007.

Paul sits on the board of the Chicago Council on Global Affairs, the Mayor's Board of Chicago World Business, the President's Council of the University of Tokyo, CEOs Against Cancer, and the International Advisory Board of BritishAmerican Business. Additionally, he is a member of the Council on Foreign Relations as well as CEOs in Partnership for a New American Economy, which is a non-partisan coalition to address U.S. immigration issues.

A sought-after speaker, Paul has addressed audiences in more than 50 countries.

When not on an airplane, he lives in Santa Fe, New Mexico, with his wife, Louise, and family.

For further information, go to: www.beatingtheglobalodds.com

Index

Stay in touch!

Subscribe to our free Finance and Accounting eNewsletters at
www.wiley.com/enewsletters

Visit our blog: **www.capitalexchangeblog.com**

 Follow us on Twitter
@wiley_finance

 "Like" us on Facebook
www.facebook.com/wileyglobalfinance

 Find us on LinkedIn
Wiley Global Finance Group